STRANGERS

AT HOME

STRANGERS

AT HOME

Essays on the Effects of
Living Overseas and Coming
"Home" to a Strange Land

Edited by Carolyn D. Smith

ALETHEIA
Publications

Smith, Carolyn D.
Strangers at home: essays on the effects of living over-
seas and coming "home" to a strange land

Library of Congress Catalog Card Number: 96-85760
ISBN: 0-9639260-4-7

Copyeditor: Leslie Bernstein
Cover design: Jackie Frant
Interior design and composition: Guy J. Smith

Aletheia Publications, 38-15 Corporal Kennedy St.,
Bayside, NY 11361

Printed in Canada
10 9 8 7 6 5 4 3

Contents

Foreword

THIS IS A COLLECTION of essays about the experiences of children growing up in cultures not their own. Some are written by parents and some by the children as adults and a few by individuals doing research in this aspect of child rearing. With the exception of the elegantly designed study of military children and families by Morten Ender, the essays are largely personal. The writers share memories and impressions of growing up in different countries. The book is a rich source of advice for people who pursue this lifestyle.

As a child psychiatrist working with people who move every two or three years to different countries, I am often asked by parents how this lifestyle affects children. Do children raised on the move have more psychological problems than those who stay in one place? How do they turn out as adults? I answer that the outcome depends on the child and the family more than on the country and the move. There are no controlled, prospective longitudinal studies on the adult outcomes of children raised overseas. Until there are, predictions and advice should be given in the

context of individual experiences and judged by
what makes good sense. Most important, one
should keep in mind that there are many ways to
raise children and that children are resilient and
tend to grow up more healthy than otherwise, especially in families that understand them.

In this one book there is a range of opinions about the adult outcome of children raised in
foreign cultures. Ruth Useem and Ann Cottrell state
that such children rarely adjust fully. Linda Bell
reports that her interviewees have stable lifestyles and that their roots are in people rather than
places. The missionary environment Ruth Van
Reken grew up in offered a sense of orderliness
and security, valuable elements in any childhood.
Jody Merrill-Foster says that her children were
happier on the plane than in America. Clare
Kittredge finds examples of both kinds of outcomes. There are some who find a place once they
are "home" but retain the sense of specialness that
comes from having lived in another culture, and
there are a few who do not feel at home in any
place. All agree that the experience of living in
another country is never forgotten.

All children need a sense of place and continuity. David Pollock offers helpful suggestions
to families about maintaining ties with the home
country, and Linda Bell points out that a sense of
origin can come from a powerful figure, in her case
a grandmother who was visited only infrequently.
Continuity in education is important, and Kay
Branaman Eakin offers excellent concrete advice
on what can be done to ease reentry for returning students. Norma McCaig also explains what

parents can do and focuses on the benefits that come to children from living with diversity. Carolyn Smith observes something that rings true to all of us working in this field—the ease with which children raised in other cultures have friendships throughout their lives with people from different countries.

Morten Ender's essay approaches the subject from a research perspective and draws conclusions reinforced by statistics. He reviews the literature about the effects of military life on the family and correctly, in my opinion, points to two critical factors that determine poor adjustment: the absence of the parent from the home and frequent moves. He states that the long-term effects of this lifestyle are not known, but it is clear that the experience is not lost. I share his conclusion that these children show tolerance for other cultures, are flexible, enjoy foreign languages, and for the most part have positive educational experiences.

The essays describe people who are trying to make sense of the overseas experience. The children feel a sense of specialness, and some find comfort in joining organizations that help them validate their feelings and integrate childhood experiences into adult identities. But is this not the goal of everyone, to place closure on childhood in order to understand and accept one's adult self? My hunch is that children raised overseas are not better adjusted or less adjusted than those who remained at home. The experience is potentially enriching, and when an adult has problems it is not easy to demonstrate that they are a result of this type of childhood. There are many determinants of the healthy adult personality, and research in child development now focuses as much on what keeps children healthy as on what makes them ill. Fortunately, children are resilient and, with sensible parenting and reasonable communities and schools, most do quite well. I think that the range of observations expressed by the authors of these essays demonstrates the wide variability in adult outcomes of childhood experiences. How the life is led is one of the most critical determinants, and the authors' many good and practical suggestions will help the thoughtful parent who is wondering what to do next.

— Elmore F. Rigamer, M.D., M.P.A.
Medical Director,
U.S. State Department and the
Foreign Service

Introduction

THIS IS A BOOK for and about Americans who
spent some or all of their childhood years over
seas. Variously known as overseas brats, third culture kids, global nomads, military brats, missionary kids,
and absentee Americans, among other terms, these
individuals have all shared the experiences of life as
an expatriate, one or more "reentries" or returns "home"
to the United States (or other country of origin), and
the long-term process of readjustment to American
society and culture. Those experiences have shaped
their personalities and outlook on life, so much so
that there is a growing body of literature that describes salient characteristics of this population subgroup and examines the unique problems and
benefits of an expatriate childhood.

This is not to say that a sojourn overseas does
not affect those who live abroad for the first time as
adults. Indeed, for some people the impact of overseas living can be even greater in adulthood than in
childhood, and their lives may be dramatically
changed as a result. Perhaps the most interesting
accounts of such experiences are provided by adults
who have raised children while living overseas, for
they have seen expatriate life and reentry both
through their own eyes and through their children's.

This collection of articles and essays presents several perspectives on overseas life and its effects. Some, written by individuals who lived overseas in childhood, describe their experiences and how they were affected by them. Some selections were contributed by social scientists who have conducted surveys and observations of "third culture kids" of all ages. They identify some of the key characteristics of this subset of the population, and some offer suggestions that can be helpful to parents wishing to ease their children's sometimes difficult transition to life at "home" in the United States. Other selections are by individuals who may or may not have lived overseas in childhood, but who have done so as adults. They portray some of the joys and hardships of family life in an expatriate community.

In the first essay, "Growing Up Global," Clare Kittredge offers a journalist's-eye view of what life was like for American children living overseas in the 1960s. Her article pinpoints some of the most salient qualities of the expatriate lifestyle—frequent moves, exposure to many cultures and languages, occasional danger, stark scenes of poverty and suffering, a sense of adventure, and more.

In the next selection, "Adult Third Culture Kids," Ruth Hill Useem and Ann Baker Cottrell describe the origins of the concept of a third culture and the term *third culture kid* (abbreviated throughout the book as TCK). They also present the key findings of an ongoing study of adult TCKs (ATCKs)—their strong sense of differentness, their efforts to fit in, their educational attainments and career achievements—ending with an overall portrait of ATCKs as a group.

A particularly intense version of the TCK experience is seen in accounts by people who attended boarding schools overseas. That experience is vividly portrayed by Paul Seaman in his essay, "Rediscovering a Sense of Place." Seaman, who spent many years at Murree Christian School in northern Pakistan, describes boarding school life and the confusion he felt upon returning "home" to an unfamiliar country. He also describes the sense of discovery and relief he experienced upon realizing that he is part of a community of people with similar backgrounds and a similar world view.

The difficulty of going "home" after living overseas, especially for teenagers, is explored in detail by Kay Branaman Eakin in her essay, "You Can't Go Home Again." She points out that cross-cultural research indicates that the return to one's country of origin can be more difficult than initial entry into an overseas setting. She offers some suggestions for parents who wish to ease their children's transition back into American society.

In "Religious Culture Shock," Ruth Van Reken describes another kind of experience that can have deep and lasting effects. Her essay explores the soul-searching that missionary kids undergo in attempting to adjust to a culture that is, for the most part, far more secular than those in which they grew up.

Norma McCaig also addresses the issue of "coming home" in her essay, "Understanding Global Nomads." She points to the valuable skills acquired by children in overseas settings—especially language and social skills—and to some unique characteristics of internationally mobile families. She also presents some strategies parents can adopt to guide their children as they attempt to cope with the stresses of coming "home" to an unfamiliar place.

Having read these first few essays, the reader is invited to pause and enjoy Amy Rukea Stempel's poem, "Rail Ways." For those who have spent much time traveling, her words are a reminder of the mixed emotions that arise as an ever-changing landscape rolls by.

As mentioned earlier, several social scientists have focused their research efforts on the nature and consequences of a mobile childhood. Among them is Morten Ender. Born into a military family, he has long been interested in the key characteristics of the military lifestyle and their impact on children. In "Growing Up in the Military" he outlines some of the long-term effects, both positive and negative, of growing up in a military family.

Jody Merrill-Foster's article, "Behind the Swinging Door," illustrates the perspective of a Foreign Service wife. In the 1960s, when she and her husband first lived overseas, the role of a Foreign Service wife was essentially limited to learning the language and culture, running the household, and "representational entertaining." Although she was unable to find a job, she developed her skills as a writer and observer, skills that are clearly evident in her description of her children's reactions to overseas life.

Linda Bell has also lived overseas as an adult with a young child. Her daughter's query about what language is spoken in the United States was the catalyst for an extended inquiry into the meaning and consequences of growing up without "roots," at least in the traditional sense of the term. She explored this question in numerous interviews with people who had lived overseas in childhood. Some of the themes emerging from those interviews are described in her article, "Rolling Stones Smooth Out Nicely."

Perhaps the most basic issue facing Americans who have lived overseas has to do with cultural (and national) identity. Barbara Schaetti addresses this issue in her article, "Phoenix Rising:

A Question of Cultural Identity." Noting that many global nomads cringe when they are referred to as "American," she explores some of the reasons for this phenomenon, focusing on the cultural marginality experienced by those who are exposed to two or more cultural traditions.

In the next selection, "World Citizens and 'Rubber-Band Nationality,'" Carolyn Smith speculates on the causes and consequences of the expanded view of national identity so often found among people who have lived overseas for a significant period, either in childhood or as adults. She uses the phrase "rubber-band nationality" to describe the elastic sense of nationality expressed by many expatriates and returnees.

In the final selection, "Where Will I Build My Nest?," sociologist David C. Pollock broadens the scope of the discussion to include people of many different nationalities who have shared the experience of trying to figure out where "home" is. He points to the universality of the identity crisis experienced by young people in internationally mobile families. While noting that the response will vary according to the individual's personality and perceptions, he describes four basic categories of responses that occur frequently among the TCKs he has encountered in the course of his extensive travels as a cross-cultural consultant.

These articles, of course, only begin to reflect the complexity of the experience summarized in the book's title, *Strangers at Home*. More, and more indepth, analysis and information can be found in the works listed in the bibliography. Also included is a list of organizations of interest to people who have lived overseas.

Growing Up Global
Clare Kittredge

*CLARE KITTREDGE grew up as a Foreign Service brat
in Europe, Southeast Asia, and the Middle East. During
the 1950s and 1960s she and her two sisters lived in
France, Vietnam (between wars), Japan, Israel, and Italy.
Raised bilingually, she spent a dozen years in the French
school system, then switched to American schools in the
latter part of high school. She came "home" to the United
States at the height of the Vietnam War to go to college.
She now lives in New Hampshire, where she has worked
for almost a decade as a regular contributor to the Boston Globe.*

IN THE LAST WILD moments of the Vietnam
War, the image of Americans fleeing by heli-
copter from the roof of the U.S. Embassy in Saigon
was broadcast around the world. For many, the impact was brutal. But my mind slid to quiet streets
between a palace and a zoo, where eight small
houses slumped in smells of flowers, rain, decay.
Blue-headed lizards lazed in long-armed trees. Pa-
ralysis by heat.

Vietnam was our second post, a two-year stop
between France and Japan, one of a string of countries my sisters and I called home as children of the
United States Foreign Service.

In Saigon, where we lived between 1957 and
1959, our lives revolved around the U.S. Embassy,
where my father worked; the compound near President Ngo Dinh Diem's palace, where we lived; the
Couvent des Oiseaux, where we went to school; a
rain-streaked colonial pool festooned with bouga-
invillea; and a stable where tiny horses seemed to
die regularly of worms.

The United States was a faraway place whose
manifestations included gum and soft drinks, tired
movies shown at birthday parties, a few American
businessmen, a handful of U.S. military people, a
little PX, and a dispensary where a nurse doled out
candy in exchange for the pain of shots. It was a
place we glimpsed every two and a half years on
"home leave," when we stared at doughy Americans
and chattering TV and visited large numbers of relatives. It was a place some people missed. One Christmas in Saigon, at age eight, I watched with curiosity
as teenage girls across the compound from us made
cocoa in the oppressive heat, jitterbugged with one
another, and talked wistfully about "home."

But home to us was the compound where we
played in puddles filled with frogs' eggs during rainy
season. Where poinsettias bloomed and incense
burned in tiny shrines. Out on the street, ladies in
pointed hats sold soup and bananas, spoke French,
and occasionally squatted on the sidewalk to pee.
Saigon was the place where one of my sisters se-
cretly traded away all her toys. It was where our
mother told us the tale of the city mouse and the
country mouse, except that her version was about a
rat that crept through the Saigon sewers into the
president's palace. It was where we learned to swim.

* * *

EVER since John Quincy Adams accompanied his father to the Netherlands in 1779 at age eleven, the children of American diplomatic secretaries, dignitaries, and functionaries have been hauled all over the world while their parents staffed the posts that make foreign affairs possible.

Things must not have been easy for diplomats' children even then. Travel was dangerous. Adams, used to relatively small-town American surroundings, was separated from his mother for several years and plunged into large, alien urban environments like Paris and London.

Due to a fear of elitism and foreign influence, State Department historian William Slany says, the diplomatic corps was an object of suspicion to members of a government founded on the belief that the common man could conduct his own affairs with kings. The diplomatic service, Slany says, was made more democratic by the formation of today's U.S. Foreign Service in 1924 and by successive reforms. Even so, he says, today, unlike those of some other countries, U.S. Embassy postings are scattered worldwide, and tours of duty are kept short.

Today, about 15,000 to 20,000 children of more than 8,000 American Foreign Service employees are arriving, taking off, watching Earth's textures go by; sleeping in airports, fighting jet lag in strange hotels; adjusting to new schools, making new friends and leaving others; learning firsthand about war, Third World poverty, and the effects of U.S. foreign policy; getting through natural and political cataclysms as they grow up in 256 posts all over the world; and coming home.

* * *

LOOKING out the windows of the Istanbul-Ankara express for the first time, Bernard (Barney) Dale was entranced by sights he'd seen only in his elementary school geography book—"women in Turkish peasant dresses, men driving solid-wheel ox-drawn carts, scenes from the Bronze Age."

Already he had lived in Ottawa, Paris, London, and Washington. But in 1960 his parents were stationed at the U.S. Embassy in Ankara, and he was plunged into the Middle East. He was eleven.

"The whole Muslim culture and religion were very strange," he says. "I fell in love with it." As a little boy, he was tutored in Turkish and learned German at the Deutsche Botschaftsschule, a German embassy school near his house. He collected Turkish stamps, Roman coins, ancient ceramic pots. During Ramadan, the Muslim holy month of fasting, he visited Turkish villages with sun-baked mud houses, fascinated by such apparent oddities as piles of sheep hearts from freshly sacrificed sheep steaming in the early morning sun.

Like many Turks, he drank real fruit juice instead of American-style soft drinks. He did not watch TV. In 1963, he remembers, he heard about President John F. Kennedy's assassination over the radio.

But Ankara was the site of a large U.S. military presence. "Some of the Americans seemed to scorn the Turks. They thought they were filthy and poor. They secluded themselves and preferred hot dogs to kebabs."

Once, a drunken Air Force sergeant climbed a minaret and tried to call the faithful to prayer, Dale says. Another wrapped himself in the Turkish flag and later threw it in the garbage. American tourists with Bermuda shorts, Hawaiian shirts, and piles of cash struck him as boors.

Yet in the early 1960s the Turkish man-on-the-street admired the United States and wanted to emulate Americans, Dale says. "They wanted anything American—watches, lighters, clothing. They traded Roman coins for ballpoint pens. It saddened me to think they would throw away their traditional values to live in the same shoddy houses, drive the same crummy cars, and lead the same tacky lifestyle they couldn't afford."

Leading a life that challenged his own sense of the word "normal," Dale developed ambivalent feelings about apparent absolutes. "Something there is that doesn't love a wall," says Dale, borrowing a line from Robert Frost.

In 1964 his family was stationed in Tel Aviv. Israel did not have an accredited American high school, so he was sent to the American Community School in Beirut, then a serene city on the Mediterranean. Like other Arab countries, Lebanon did not recognize Israel's existence.

"In school, being from Israel was considered unspeakable—people called it 'Dixie,'" Dale says. On his way to Israel, to visit his parents in a country that officially did not exist, he rode down the Lebanese coast, through banana groves and orange orchards, past the ancient Phoenician cities of Tyre and Sidon, where the Mediterranean crashed against white cliffs and few people seemed to live.

"There was a sense of loneliness and excitement, of going to a place that was forbidden," he says. He drank tea with a border guard, crossed no man's land, a narrow strip of unoccupied land between Lebanon and Israel, and drank another cup of tea.

A train track running through no man's land had once connected Beirut to Tel Aviv but was twisted wildly out of shape. "I thought it was symbolic of the total lack of communication between these two places that existed, yet denied each other's existence," Dale says. "I still have a card that says in Arabic that I'm allowed to travel to the so-called occupied territory—Israel is not mentioned."

Dale recognizes that as a diplomatic child, he was privileged. "Only because people closed one eye could I do it," he says. "It was like being a traveler between two dimensions."

* * *

OFTEN, Foreign Service children discover that war and violence are more than abstract items in the news. Around the same time, halfway around the world, Christian Coles played with Tinkertoys while anti-imperialist Viet Cong leaflets drifted into his back yard. It was the fall of 1964.

Coles's brother Wick rode a school bus guarded by an armed Marine. Chicken wire stretched over the windows to keep out grenades. The American Community School in Saigon was ringed with barbed wire, and Marines manned machine-gun emplacements on the roof. "Home" was a fortified house with a high fence topped with broken glass. From the roof, Wick, a teenager, listened to the screams of the F-4 Phantom jets and watched American helicopters rise like birds over Saigon.

Five months later, in March 1965, the Coleses were evacuated from Saigon under jet-fighter escort. At age five, Christian was making his second circle around the world. Three years after that, he found himself going through air-raid drills at the American International School in Israel. In June 1967 he was evacuated again, for the Arab-Israeli Six-Day War. He was eight.

Insulated by his parents and his youth, Coles, like many small children, found evacuation exciting. But his mother was nervous leaving Saigon, and other people were reportedly hysterical. Some Foreign Service children are said to have been deeply disturbed by close brushes with political and social violence in such places as Central America and South Africa.

Barney Dale was marked by what he saw in Israel. He remembers surveying the hulks of tanks rusting in the Negev desert and the military hardware decomposing on the Golan Heights after the Six-Day War. In some parts of the world, he says, "war was a neighborhood thing. It was close. The closest most Americans come to it is paying taxes to support it."

* * *

THERE is nothing quite like the feeling of being whisked about in an embassy car and seeing tiny hands the size of your own trying to reach through the window at a stop light, or trying to finish everything on your plate when ten pairs of hungry eyes are watching.

Growing up in East Pakistan (now Bangladesh) and West Pakistan (now Pakistan), Stephanie Turco had gotten used to being a well-fed American child amid great human suffering. But nothing prepared her for Calcutta, where her family was posted in 1975, when she was nine years old.

"India is everything," she says,

the humidity, the crowds. Your senses are on at full speed. On a typical day in Calcutta, the streets are filled with people—beggars eating garbage, people sleeping, people who are born and die on the streets. During the monsoons, the streets flood and people live on floating contraptions in the middle of the street.

Close to her parents' apartment in downtown Calcutta was a huge, reeking garbage pit the size of a building, she says. Vultures picked at carcasses while beggars picked recyclable items and food from the garbage and pawned the items at a nearby market. Stray dogs, cats, and cows wandered streets haunted by lepers and mutilated, blind, and starving people.

She talks about the endless inoculations, the precautions against intestinal parasites—boiling the water, not eating lettuce—the seemingly endless amount of time it took to go to the Woodstock School, an international Christian boarding school in Mussoorie, northern India, where she spent several years. In school she studied the Indian struggle for independence, and both Indian and American history. On vacations she toured ancient archaeological sites with her parents and visited the tombs of British soldiers in old Calcutta graveyards.

Then she moved. In early 1978, pro-Soviet leftists took power in a coup in Kabul, Afghanistan. Turco's family arrived in September of that year. Nine months later, on Valentine's Day 1979, her eighth-grade class at the American International School ended early.

"Something was wrong," she remembers. At home, halfway across the little city ringed with snow-covered Himalayan peaks, she found her mother crying. Ambassador Adolph (Spike) Dubs had been kidnapped by a terrorist posing as a policeman and killed.

Turco was fourteen. "It was scary," she says, "because the adults were so shaken. Some AID [Agency for International Development] families were shipped out. Through the spring and summer, the situation got worse." In July her family was evacuated to New Delhi, while her father completed his tour in Kabul. In December, one month after Iranians took sixty-three Americans hostage at the American Embassy in Tehran, the Russians invaded Afghanistan.

Dr. Elmore F. Rigamer, a State Department psychiatrist assigned to treat U.S. Embassy children in Kabul after the ambassador's death, found that some children had woven wildly distorted accounts of his assassination. Some went over and over the gruesome details of his death. Others worried that it would happen to them. Often, parental reassurance didn't work, he found, because some parents, in their haste to restore calm, did not allow their children to express anxiety.

Today, all U.S. Foreign Service employees going overseas are required to attend a two-day State Department seminar called "Coping with Violence Abroad," in which they learn ways to avoid such things as kidnappings, hostage takings, and terrorist acts, and how to manage stress. "There are places where Americans remain popular overseas," says Barbara Hoganson, coordinator of the seminar, "but some groups worldwide do pose a threat to people with government connections."

"Everyone worries about violence and terrorism overseas nowadays," Turco says. "It's a real change for Foreign Service people. There are some posts now like Beirut and Kabul where wives and children just don't go."

* * *

GROWING up as unofficial minirepresentatives of the United States under the scrutiny of a constantly changing group of foreigners, diplomats' children develop their own slant on the world.

David Pollock, who gives seminars for diplomatic and other families posted overseas, calls them third culture kids—those who, like the children of missionaries, businesspeople, and some military people, have integrated the cultures of home and several host countries into a "third" culture. Third culture kids, he says, tend to speak several languages, have cross-cultural skills, and have a three-dimensional world view.

"They know that when a mother's child is dying in Seoul, Korea, she goes through the same pain as a mother whose child is dying in New York City," Pollock says. And, he says, they tend to resent American ethnocentrism and news reports that focus on American casualties alone, portray the United States as all-important, or present 1776 as Day One. Often, they are acutely aware of the difference between this country's self-image and foreigners' views of American actions overseas.

When Foreign Service children return to the United States for high school or college, he says, many have no adjustment problems and slide right into the American scene and put down roots. But sometimes their crazy-quilt childhoods make them "privy to many cultures and owners of none," Pollock says. They lack a geographical sense of home and may experience a "migratory urge" in career and marriage.

"Knowing a culture is a little like Trivial Pursuit," Pollock says.

You don't study it, you live through it. You collect lots of information—values, bits and pieces of history, the names of athletes, in-jokes, humor, code words—and store it away. Then, during personal exchanges, you dip back into the data bank and pull them out and make connections with other people.

Knowing little about American TV, politics, and music, armed only with an image of the United States assembled from home-leave impressions, their parents' memories, and popular magazines, some returnees feel culturally off-balance when they get "home." Pollock calls it "reverse culture shock."

* * *

BARNEY DALE spent four years at Kenyon College, in Gambier, Ohio, in the late 1960s, then taught English for a year at his former high school in Beirut, where he marched against American aid to Israel. When he came back to the United States in 1971, his teaching deferment had ended. His draft lottery number was low. Over in Vietnam he saw another traditional Third World culture being laid waste. "I knew there was absolutely no way I was going to go."

The Fourth of July 1971, he recalls, was "Honor America Day." "In Washington, tear gas and marijuana smoke wafted through the air. There was a big celebration on the Mall with millions of freaks, yippies hitting the food stands to 'liberate' the food, and straights who had come to hear Bob Hope."

Dale was twenty-two, a gangly blond in a blue work shirt and jeans. "Across the Mall an older woman saw me—another long-haired hippie freak—and said, "If you don't like it, why don't you leave?"

"'I am,' I told her, 'I am.'" He got into his '65 Ford Falcon, drove across the United States to Canada, and renounced his American citizenship.

He was stateless for several years, then became a Canadian citizen. In 1976 he married an American. But when he came back to the United States five years ago and went through a standard background check as part of his application for "resident alien" status, he says, he was allowed back in not because of his wife's nationality but because he was from a diplomatic family. "They looked at me and said, 'Oh, another diplomatic brat,'" he says with a sigh. "'He can have his green card if he wants.'"

Christian Coles had lived in seven overseas posts—Japan, Taiwan, Hong Kong, India, Vietnam, Israel, and Turkey—when he came back to the United States in 1977 to go to Boston University. He had been around the world five times, attended half a dozen schools, spoke Hindi slang, French, and Hebrew, and had a range of interests. But when he returned to the States, he realized that overseas he had grown up blissfully unaware of the significance of being black.

"The big question is, 'What are you?'" he says.

> Overseas, I was an American. People either liked me or they didn't like me. And we looked forward to new people, new places, new foods, new games. Here, the whole perspective is different. People look for classifications, and they tend to fear change or difference.

Stephanie Turco was not prepared for the U.S. social scene when she went to the University of Maryland in 1983. For one thing, she wore a nose ring, a tiny diamond stud twisted into one nostril. It was beautiful, she says. "I'd had it done in India, but at the University of Maryland they thought I was from outer space. It was too bizarre for them to see a Western woman with that thing in her face.

"I wanted to fit in, so I started wearing it only at night. But my memories of India are very special, and nobody shared them," she says. "Typically, freshman year I'd go to a party and people would say, 'Where are you from?' and I'd say, 'India.'

"'Indiana? Oh, I got a cousin in Indiana.'

"'No, India—south Asia.'

And they'd get a blank expression on their face and walk away. Some people thought I was boasting—they were intimidated. Some people didn't know where India was. A lot of them just weren't all that interested. So I stopped telling people where I came from. I found myself socializing with outcasts. I felt like the only person in the world who'd ever left the eastern shore of Maryland.

"A lot of [Foreign Service] kids tell me they just don't like the U.S.," says Teresa Lauderdale, a Foreign Service child who grew up in South America and Europe in the 1960s and 1970s. Many are surprised by the drug scene, urban violence, Americans' lack of interest in geography and foreign languages. Consumption, unconscious waste, the size of supermarkets, are all shocking to children who have grown up in countries where people make the most of limited resources. "Once in a while," Lauderdale says, "parents let kids go back to posts, but you can't really go back because you can't go back in time."

* * *

SLOWLY, the government has been responding to the needs of Foreign Service children. Ten years ago the State Department formed the Family Liaison Office, which provides support services for Foreign Service families. In the early 1980s it started Transition to Washington Workshop, a reentry program for Foreign Service families. In 1983 several Foreign Service children, with the support of a few groups, including the Association of American Foreign Service Women, founded Around the World in a Lifetime (AWAL), a teenager-run support group for returnees.

Other groups are getting off the ground. In 1986 the daughter of an American businessman who grew up in the Far East, Norma McCaig, founded Global Nomads International, a support group for the children of missionaries, businesspeople, military personnel, and Foreign Service people. Mu Kappa—Multicultural Kids—now represents the children of missionaries. Both McCaig and Pollock, the sociologist, want to hold "Woodstock" reunions for third culture kids.

"We recognize that it's a changed world," says Maryann Minutillo, education counselor at the State Department's Family Liaison office, "and that Foreign Service families need our help."

"We live in an age of increased global interdependence," says McCaig. "We want to encourage global nomads to use their skills to stress the positive and enriching aspects of cultural diversity." Criticism is not unpatriotic, she says. The idea, Pollock says, is for third culture kids to become "bridges" to the future, not an alienated resource.

* * *

TODAY, Stephanie Turco, twenty-two, is working toward her master's degree in Arab studies at

Georgetown University and plans to move to the Arab world. Lauderdale, twenty-six, is a tourism consultant in Washington, D.C.

Armed with a master's degree in journalism, Christian Coles, twenty-nine, wants to cover international science and technology issues for newspapers and television, and occasionally works with the Center for War, Peace, and the News Media, in New York City.

Barney Dale, thirty-nine, is raising two children. He says he enjoys being a househusband and developing real estate in a small North Carolina town. But he doesn't think he'll ever settle down. "[Growing up overseas] turned me into an eternal tourist," he says. "I move every four years."

Nor does he feel he has one nationality. "There's a great line by Tennyson," he says.

> 'I am a part of all that I have met.' You live that line a lot if you're exposed to different cultures. You become part of all of them. Now, I'm very much part Lebanese and part Turk. I think of myself as a North American. And I find it almost easier to be an American as a Canadian.

* * *

THE Foreign Service children I talked to are fiercely attached to their childhoods. "I didn't feel I fit in here as a child," says Helen Chapin Metz, fifty-nine, who grew up in Southeast Asia, Europe, and Central America, "but by the time I got through college I was over that, and I realized what I'd gained was far more important than what I'd missed."

What did we learn? Who knows—just that somewhere, a blue-headed lizard is chirping on a tree limb, that someone is comfortable with the wail of the Muslim call to prayer, and that somewhere, a little kid the age we once were is sleeping in a cardboard box and calling that home.

Adult
Third Culture Kids*
Ruth Hill Useem and
Ann Baker Cottrell

RUTH HILL USEEM is professor emeritus of sociology and education at Michigan State University. She and her husband, John, originated the term third culture kids, and they have conducted extensive research on adults who spent many of their childhood years in cultures other than that of their "home" or passport country. She has published numerous articles in sociological and anthropological journals and has served as a consultant, keynote speaker, and workshop presenter at overseas schools operated by the State Department and the Department of Defense.

ANN BAKER COTTRELL is a professor of sociology and assistant director of the Office for International Programs at San Diego State University. Her fascination with internationally mobile lifestyles began with her own first overseas experience, a junior year abroad in Scotland. Her research focus on transnational families eventually grew into a study of South Asians married to Westerners living in India, the United States, and Britain. Her advisors and mentors were John and Ruth Hill Useem, with whom she has collaborated in the study of third culture

* This is a revision of five short articles that appeared in NewsLinks, The Newspaper of the International Schools Services, vols. 7 and 8.

kids described in this article. She has also conducted a comparative study of the reentry experiences of women students attending U.S. and Italian universities.

MANY PEOPLE HAVE ASKED the origin and meaning of the term *third culture* as we use it in *third culture kids*, or TCKs, and, by extrapolation, in *adult TCKs*. To clear up one confusion, "third culture" is not synonymous with "third world" or with C. P. Snow's Third Culture. However, they are all related in that they were early attempts to describe a major shift in the relationships among the peoples of the globe in the mid-twentieth century.

The ending of colonialism, the dramatic increase in science and technology, and the rise of two relatively new world powers—the United States and the Soviet Union—all combined to produce major changes in the patterns of movement of human beings around the world and the purposes for which they were entering other societies.

It was some forty years ago, in 1952, that I [Ruth Hill Useem] had my first cross-cultural encounter outside the United States. My husband and I, accompanied by our three sons (aged four, five, and ten), went to India for a year to study the roles of Indians who had been abroad for higher education. Five years later we returned to India (again with our children) for a year's field study of Americans living and working there, primarily as foreign service officers, missionaries, technical aid workers, businesspeople, educators, and media representatives. We also looked at the schools that were set up to educate minor dependents accompanying their parents abroad.

In summarizing our observations, we began to use *third culture* as a generic term to cover the lifestyles created, shared, and learned by people who are in the process of relating their societies, or aspects thereof, to each other. The term *third culture kids*, or TCKs, was coined to refer to the children who accompany their parents into another society.

What we had observed in India was happening all over the world. In 1960, the U.S. Census published its first-ever census of Americans overseas. There was scarcely a country without a contingent of Americans. Some of the more than 200,000 American children of school age living overseas were attending newly established Department of Defense schools. Others were enrolled in makeshift schools assisted by the Department of State. Missionary groups tended to set up their own schools, and oil companies set up their "camp schools."

As early as the 1960s and with increasing frequency, changes were occurring in the overseas schools and the American communities abroad that foreshadowed the major restructuring of the world's political economy in the 1990s. Two illustrations will suffice. The first was the United States' recognition of China, which meant that in a short span of time American military personnel and their dependents were withdrawn from Taiwan. The second, one of the most dramatic and far-reaching changes ever, was the Vietnam War and its disastrous close. How do TCKs experience these world changes, in which their parents are often intimately involved? How are these experiences reassessed? How do adults who spent their early years abroad ("adult TCKs") in a country in which they had a happy and rewarding childhood reassess that nation-state when it becomes the enemy? There also have been major shifts in American life. Do adult TCKs evaluate them differently than Americans reared within the United States?

To explore these and other related questions, we undertook a research project on adult TCKs who are at least twenty-five, who currently reside in the United States, and who spent at least one school-age year abroad as the minor dependent of an American parent. We distributed a twenty-four-page questionnaire to these adult TCKs.

Over 700 individuals ranging in age from 25 to 90 returned the questionnaire. The following analysis is based on the responses of 604 of them, all of whom had lived abroad as children in the post-World War II period. Some of these TCKs spent most of their childhood and teen years overseas, while others were abroad only one year, usually with parents who were on academic sabbaticals. The majority of the participants in this study, however, spent a significant part of their early years outside the United States. Nearly three-quarters lived abroad both as preteens and as teenagers; half spent nine or more school years abroad. While the majority lived in one or two countries, some moved a great deal and one lived in eight different countries while growing up.

From previous research, we had concluded that the sponsor—that is, the organization for which their parents worked abroad—made a difference in the type of family life and schooling that minor dependents experienced abroad. The third culture of the diplomatic community differs from that found on a military base. The third culture of businesspeople abroad impinges differently on the daily lives of their children than does that of missionaries on their offspring. Segments of the host nation who interact with some foreigners may not even be aware of others. What we did not know was whether or not these somewhat different third-culture experiences resulted in different trajectories in the TCKs' adult lives.

To look at these dimensions, we included in our sample men and women whose parents were

overseas with the military (30 percent of this sample),
the State Department (23 percent), religious organizations (17 percent), business enterprises (16 percent), and a miscellany of other sponsors such as
colleges and universities, news media, and the United
Nations (14 percent). Some of our more striking findings are described here.

Delayed Adolescence

ONLY one out of every ten of our adult TCKs say
that they feel completely attuned to everyday life in
the United States. The other 90 percent say that they
are more or less "out of synch" with their age group
throughout their lifetime.

Being out of step with those around them is
especially noticeable—and painful—in the late teens
and twenties, when choice of mate, occupation, and
lifestyle are being worked out. Some young adult
TCKs strike their close peers, parents, and counselors as being self-centered adolescents, as having
champagne tastes on beer incomes (or no incomes),
as not being able to make up their minds about what
they want to do with their lives, where they want to
live, and whether or not they want to "settle down,
get married, and have children." They have what
some call prolonged adolescence.

Others do what those around them are do-
ing. They marry at the appropriate time, get a "good"
job, have a child or children, take on a mortgage,
and then throw it all over at age forty in order to
take a job overseas. Some resign from high-paying
positions and return to college to be retrained for a
low-paying teaching job. Still others withdraw from
all social contact because of extreme depression or
because they have come into an inheritance and are

quite happy doing nothing but writing French poetry or traveling to all the places they have never
been. This is what some have called delayed adolescence.

How long does it take for TCKs to become
adjusted to American life? The majority of our adult
TCKs report mild to severe difficulties with what have
been called "reentry problems" or "reverse culture
shock." Throughout their lifetimes there are subtle
differences between them and the American generation that came into adulthood in the same historical
period. Not being like their peers is usually of great
import to them in their late teens and twenties, but
its centrality decreases as they grow older.

The answer to the question of how long it
takes them to adjust to American life is: they never
adjust. They adapt, they find niches, they take risks,
they fail and pick themselves up again. They suc-
ceed in jobs they have created to fit their particular
talents, they locate friends with whom they can share
some of their interests, but they resist being encapsulated. They are loners without being particularly
lonely. Their camouflaged exteriors and understated
ways of presenting themselves hide rich inner lives,
remarkable talents, and, often, strongly held contradictory opinions on the world at large and the
world at hand.

Fitting In

ON the surface, most adult TCKs conform to what is
going on around them in such a way that attention
is not drawn to them. As they meet new people and
new situations, they are slow to commit themselves
until they have determined what behavior is ex-

pected. If what is expected is unacceptable or incomprehensible, they will quietly withdraw rather than make fools of themselves or hurt the feelings of others.

Their bland and unremarkable exteriors, however, belie not only depths of feelings, but also considerable talents and a wealth of memories of other countries and places, including the expatriate communities in which they have lived and in which they continue to take an interest. They also have a fresh perspective on the American scene, which they are learning about throughout their lives.

And of course, they are not callow youths. They are extremely complex people who are weaving together their memories in a rapidly changing present in anticipation of an uncertain future. No two adult TCKs come up with identical ways of putting their lives together, but they are actively creating provisional answers to some of the major and minor problems that face human beings every day in this complex world. Their prolonged or delayed adolescent behavior is usually a marker that adult TCKs are trying to bring order out of the chaotic nature of their lives.

Education

ONE characteristic of adult TCKs that stands out is that the overwhelming majority of them are committed to continuing their education beyond high school. Only 21 percent of the American adult population (24 percent of men and 18 percent of women) have graduated from a four-year college. In sharp contrast, 45 percent of adult TCKs have earned at least a bachelor's degree, and half of this group have gone on to earn master's and doctoral degrees, including law and medical degrees. Less than 2 percent stopped with a high school diploma and took no advanced training. It would seem that teachers and counselors in the overseas schools, as well as parents, must have been doing a lot right over the last fifty years to have such unusual long-term results.

Most respondents say that their third culture childhood experiences affected their college choices and experiences; 43 percent say greatly, 28 percent say somewhat. Most commonly, the experience influenced what they studied. A quarter of the sample chose majors that were obviously international in content (e.g., foreign languages, anthropology, international relations). For many others the choice of a major was influenced by their overseas experiences. For example, some who chose biology had been captivated by early exposure to African wildlife; historians and artists cited their exposure to European art and historical sites as influences; pre-med, nursing, and economics majors wanted to help people they had known in less developed nations. Still others sought mainly to "get abroad again" and so majored in teaching, international relations, or international business. In addition to studying many subjects connected to international interests, over a quarter have studied abroad since high school. For some, a study-abroad program was a factor in the choice of a college.

A considerable proportion of the young adult TCKs change colleges and/or majors two or three times. Others drop out, as they put it, to "take advantage of opportunities" that happen to come up. Occasionally they drop out because a course of study is beyond their capacity, but more often they feel

that their overseas schooling and experience put
them ahead of their peers (and even their teachers).

Career Achievements

ONE of the most notable characteristics of ATCKs is
their high occupational achievement; this reflects their
high educational achievement. The majority—over 80
percent—are professionals, executives, or manag-
ers. Their occupational choices reflect a continued
love of learning, interest in helping, and desire for
independence and flexibility. The most common occupational field reported by these ATCKs is education—many are teachers, professors, or administrators—followed by those working in professional
settings such as medical or legal fields and those
who are self-employed; many of the latter are presi-
dents of their own companies. One won't find many
ATCKs in large corporations or government. The
small number in this sample who have government
jobs are in the Foreign Service or AID, or in branches
such as the Bureau of Wildlife and Fisheries or the
national parks. Although they may have been influenced by their parents' work overseas, they generally have not followed in their parents' footsteps.
Only a small percentage of these respondents, for
example, have chosen careers in the military or as
missionaries.

Regardless of their career choice, most have
incorporated an international dimension in their
work lives. For some, jobs have been highly international, such as working overseas, collaborating with
international colleagues, or advising international
students. Others weave an international dimension
into their work; a teacher, for example, enlivens her

social studies class with tales and photos of her Brazilian childhood.

A Portrait of ATCKs

TO explore feelings of connection, alienation, and/
or rootlessness and assess cross-culturally relevant
skills and behaviors, respondents were asked to indicate whether they agreed or disagreed with a list
of statements. Because globally mobile individuals
are often able to understand and appreciate more
than one point of view, and because such individuals are more comfortable with ambiguity than most,
we also gave them the opportunity to check "both."
A general portrait of ATCKs may be drawn by looking at the statements with which over half agreed.
(The percent agreeing, at least in part, with each
statement would be higher if we included those who
answered "both.")

1. *ATCKs are internationally experienced and*
continue their international involvement. ATCKs build
on a foundation of international awareness, having been socialized in a third culture for all or part
of their preadult lives. Nine out of ten report having more understanding and awareness of other
peoples and cultures than most Americans, but
most also report that their international skills and
knowledge are underutilized. More than two-thirds
say that maintaining an international dimension in
their lives is important to them. They work toward
that goal in numerous ways in addition to the international dimensions of their education and careers mentioned above. Most keep informed about
the places they have lived abroad. Most would like
to revisit the countries they lived in and most would

like to live abroad again, although not necessarily in the places where they lived as children. Consistent with their general interest in going abroad, most keep a current passport.

Their behavior supports this stated interest in maintaining an international dimension in their lives. The great majority have traveled abroad as adults. Most say they welcome opportunities to meet foreigners, and they do; over 90 percent have at least yearly contact with people from other countries. For nearly a quarter, such association occurs at least once a month—daily for some. A majority also report some, although often infrequent, contact with people they knew as children abroad. Increasingly popular are school reunions that validate the third culture and TCK identity. Some also report that in their interaction with Americans they are seen as knowledgeable about countries where they have lived and that they may be called upon to give talks or interviews or to write articles. They also share elements of overseas cultures through home decor.

A characteristic that distinguishes ATCKs from most Americans and facilitates their interaction with foreigners is their ability to communicate in other languages. Fully three-quarters of the respondents use a language other than English at least occasionally, and one in five do so regularly. Some are bilingual and work daily in a language other than English. In fact, a little over half of those who can communicate in another language use two or more.

2. ATCKs are adaptable and relate easily to a diversity of people. These respondents are comfortable in a variety of settings, as indicated by their previously noted interest in travel and living abroad and their eagerness to meet people from other countries who are in the United States. This is the "everywhere" aspect of the statement "I feel at home everywhere and nowhere," with which most agree. More than eight out of ten say that they can relate to anyone, regardless of differences such as race, ethnicity, religion, or nationality. Most establish relationships easily in new situations and have hobbies or interests that help connect them to people wherever they go.

3. *ATCKs are helpers and problem solvers.* Drawing on their own experiences in new situations, 85 percent of ATCKs say that they reach out to help those who appear unsure of themselves, especially foreigners and non-English-speaking minorities. As one respondent put it, "We know what it is like to be confused in a country where we cannot speak the language well." Moreover, most report that in situations where there is a conflict or misunderstanding, they are the ones who step in to mediate. When they themselves are facing new situations, the majority claim that they can establish relationships easily; and when confronted with unexpected or difficult situations, nearly 90 percent agree that they can usually figure out a way to handle them.

4. *ATCKs feel different but not isolated.* These respondents feel different from people who have not been overseas, and nearly half do not feel central to any group. For some, especially the recently returned, such feelings are painful and create a profound sense of isolation; this is the "nowhere" side of feeling at home everywhere and nowhere. For a few this feeling lasts a lifetime. A more common interpretation of these feelings is that ATCKs differ from other Americans not in feeling isolated but in having a broader, more global identity.

That ATCKs are not isolated and alienated, as much of the literature on the reentry period suggests, is indicated by the fact that most *disagree* with statements such as "I often feel lonely," "I am hesitant to make commitments to others," and "I feel

adrift." On the contrary, most feel that America is
the best place for them to be living and that they are
more appreciative of this country than most Americans precisely because they have lived abroad. Their
feeling of fitting in, of finding a home, is indicated by
the fact that most would find it somewhat or very
difficult to leave their present community. For some
this is a matter of obligations, but for most it is because they are integrated into community or friendship groups and, as a number of those who had an
especially mobile childhood pointed out, "I've lived
here longer than any place in my life." While saying
that they would hate to leave, the TCK background
surfaces in many who added that they could move
easily and would, in fact, enjoy meeting new people
and new challenges.

An Assessment

ANY ASSESSMENT OF THE adult lives of American
TCKs currently living in the United States must include three important points. First, in contrast to the
reentry literature that reports TCKs feeling adrift, isolated, and alienated, these respondents as a whole
do not express alienation. Their feeling of difference
from other Americans stems from their awareness
of, interest in, and desire to be connected to the larger
world community. Second, ATCKs feel enriched by
their third culture childhood. A majority agree that,
overall, such a childhood has been beneficial in their
relations with parents, siblings, spouse, and children,
as well as in social relationships, work, and higher
education. Finally, and perhaps most important,
these ATCKs, who have been geographically mobile
and have been socialized to participate in a diversity

of cultural settings, give us insights into the lifestyle and world view most appropriate to the next century—one that not only tolerates but celebrates diversity, one that is flexible and tolerant of ambiguity.

Rediscovering
a Sense of Place*
Paul Asbury Seaman

*PAUL SEAMAN is past president of Global Nomads,
Washington Area. he recently completed* Paper Airplanes
in the Himalayas: Reconstructing a Missionary Child-
hood, *which describes his experiences growing up in
Pakistan and struggling with the TCK legacy as an adult.
His articles have appeared in* Sojourners *magazine,* The
Global Nomad, *and* The Wesley Journal. *He works for
the Churches' Center for Theology and Public Policy in
Washington, D.C.*

ONE OF MY FAVORITE cartoons, from the
strip "Mr. Boffo" by Joe Martin, shows several figures leaning against the counter in a
bar and watching the TV up on the wall. One of them
is a human-size lizard in a trench coat who says,
"Which one's Gilligan?" The caption reads: *An alien
blowing his cover.* While intellectually I can appreciate the humor of this gag, its intended absurdity is a
routine experience for me—because I am a third
culture kid.

Old television programs pervade our cultural
references in the United States, whether in social

---

*Adapted from the Introduction to *Far Above the Plain: Private Pro-
files and Admissible Evidence from the First Forty Years of Murree Christian School,* edited by Paul Asbury Seaman (Pasadena, CA: William
Carey Library, 1996).

banter or in the puns of newspaper captions. Rarely does a week go by, for example, that I don't hear someone evoke the theme from "The Twilight Zone" *(doo-do doo-do, doo-do doo-do)* or make reference to "The Three Stooges." For me, raised overseas with no TV at all, these American institutions prompt about as much emotional association as entries in a traveler's phrase book. TCKs sometimes talk about their "camouflage," their ability to adopt a persona that fits in, that won't call attention to their alien reality. But often the result is a spiritual dissonance and a fragmented sense of identity. While these consequences often go unrecognized, they will certainly inhibit our ability to respond effectively to other struggles that life brings our way.

I have often felt like a refugee in my own country. However, when I finally began a conscious effort to reconcile this contradiction (in my late thirties), my heritage turned out to be quite different from the rootless, maladjusted stereotype I had accepted. The more I examined the distinctive combination of grief, alienation, and nostalgia that I associated with the TCK legacy, the more I noticed that many of these "unique" characteristics were also shared by immigrants and refugees. A greater portion of American blues, folk, and rock and roll lyrics seem to be motivated by a nagging sense of loss, a need to belong, and a desire for wholeness that is often phrased as a longing for home. Then I began to notice that the Christian sacrament of Communion—by its very name a celebration of community—expresses these same yearnings: *"Do this in remembrance of me." Share ... and be made whole. Be assured that you will find your way home.*

My own pilgrimage to remember and be reconciled with a fragmented past has been no less of a redemptive experience—and one equally dependent

on the power of community. Instinctively, I understood that to connect more fully in the present—to
feel *at home*—I had to reconnect with my past. My
"formative identity," I discovered, included not only
the experience of international living, with the at-
tendant cycles of uprooting and reentry, but also the
particulars of history and place.

   I grew up in the mountains of Pakistan, at
Murree Christian School, a boarding school for missionaries' children. Six months of the year, for ten
years, I was raised by "foster parents." Thus, for a
long time I persuaded myself that I was neither the
spiritual offspring of my father nor the cultural product of the United States of America. Gradually, sometimes awkwardly, I came to understand how much I
have been shaped by the facts listed in my passport.
Yet I am something else as well, something not defined by place or blood ties yet profoundly rooted in
geography and relationships.

   In 1957, the year I was born, Murree Christian
School officially became a cooperative, interdenominational institution for the education of missionaries'
children in Pakistan. We can surmise a great deal
about the perspective of the school's founders by looking at the times in which they lived. These missionaries came from—and still come from—independent
evangelical or fundamentalist churches, or the conservative end of the spectrum of mainline denominations. Although many of them had already been in
Pakistan for several years, they were aware of and
inevitably influenced by the dominant social forces
that were shaping the societies from which they came.
Most missionaries in the new nation of Pakistan
(founded in 1947, when the British left India) were
from the United States. And in the 1950s, conservative *Protestant* Christian culture *was* the mainstream
cultural myth in America. "Everyone" went to church,

lived in nuclear families and, with conscious effort and "right living," had equal access to the American Dream.

In 1957 Billy Graham attracted 100,000 people to an evangelical revival in New York City— the largest crowd in Yankee Stadium's history. President Dwight Eisenhower and Vice President Richard Nixon began their second term; Jimmy Hoffa was elected president of the powerful Teamsters labor union. There were still only forty-eight states; Alaska and Hawaii were admitted to the Union in 1959— the same year Fidel Castro took Cuba. Hula hoops and Marilyn Monroe were all the rage.

In reality, though, by 1957 the fifties were fast coming unraveled. That year the Ford Motor company introduced the soon-to-be-infamous Edsel, "the best engineered automobile ever designed"— and the biggest flop in automotive history. (Technology and big business were not necessarily infallible.) A discredited Senator Joseph McCarthy ended his ten-year career in the U.S. Senate, though anti-Communist hysteria would continue for several more years, fueled by the standoff in Korea and the much-publicized meeting in Peking between Soviet Premier Nikita Khrushchev and Chairman Mao Tsetung. In 1957 most Americans had not yet heard of John F. Kennedy or Vietnam; but that year heavily armed federal troops escorted black children into schools in Little Rock, Arkansas. The Montgomery, Alabama, bus boycott had begun the year before, triggering nationwide protests against segregation and beginning what would become known as the civil rights movement.

At the same time, Elvis Presley was taking the nation—and the media—by storm: for two years in a row, four of the Top Ten songs were his. Dick Clark's "American Bandstand" made its national

debut in 1957. Patsy Cline, Sam Cooke, the Everly
Brothers, Buddy Holly, Jerry Lee Lewis, Johnny
Mathis, Jimmie Rodgers, and Jackie Wilson are just
some of the singers who began their careers that
year. The year began with Harry Belafonte's "Banana Boat (Day-O)" and ended with Jerry Lee Lewis
pounding out "Great Balls of Fire." The world would
never be the same.

Antique Chevies and my own birth notwith-
standing, "57" seems to be an auspicious number.
Curiously, this year served as a defining marker, a
watershed of changing currents, for the previous two
centuries as well. In 1757, at the Battle of Plassey
outside Calcutta, the British defeated the native ruler
of Bengal, effectively establishing themselves as the
dominant power on the Indian subcontinent.

A hundred years later, the privately owned
British East India company had expanded and controlled its territory largely through the use of Indian
troops, called Sepoys, under the command of British officers. The Sepoy Mutiny—known to Indian and
Pakistani historians as the First War of Independence—began in 1857. While the rebellion was a
failure, its consequences were profound. The following year Queen Victoria abolished the East India
Company and India came under the direct adminis-
tration of the British Crown, thus ending one era and
beginning another. European *political* colonialism
(not just economic exploitation) would now dominate the globe for the next ninety years.

In 1857 Charles Dickens and Abraham Lin-
coln were forty-four years old;[1] Dwight L. Moody,
one of the century's greatest Christian evangelists,
was twenty-one. David Livingstone published his
seminal treatise on the exploration and history of
southern Africa in 1857, stimulating renewed missionary—and mercantile—interest in that continent.

Two years later Charles Darwin published his *Origin of Species.* Wheaton College, a four-year liberal arts school distinguished for its emphasis on international missions, was founded in 1860. (A hundred and thirty-five years later, it is interesting to note that more MCS graduates have enrolled at Wheaton than at any other college.) The oldest school for MKs (missionary kids) in continuous existence to the present—Woodstock School in Mussoorie, India— was three years old in 1857. The Second Great Evangelical Awakening, burning across the United States, crossed the Atlantic that year, revitalizing the missionary movement in Great Britain. As a result, the next several decades saw such a great influx of Protestant missionaries to India, China, and elsewhere that the hundred years preceding World War II have been referred to as "the missionary century."

In the past four decades the role of missionaries in Third World countries has changed dramatically. The Christian understanding of missions was transformed during the 1960s, 1970s, and 1980s nearly as much as the social and political consciousness of many nations. The new attitudes of East and West toward each other, reflecting better education and changing economic realities, has altered the global dynamic. Yet missionaries from Western countries are still a significant presence in nations of the "three-fourths world."

The care and education of missionaries' children is no quaint enterprise from the past. Today there are more than 130 schools for children of missionaries "overseas"—not including Christian academies in North America or Great Britain. No matter where they are located, these schools share a distinct subculture created by the unique combination of isolation and multicultural influence: isolated by very specific values and by the circumstances of their presence in a foreign country, yet influenced by that same foreign context and by the typically international and ecumenical character of the institutions themselves.

* * *

PAKISTAN is a "third culture *country.*" While it has been both cradle and crossroads to some of the world's greatest civilizations, it has full ownership in none of them. Its sense of belonging is with other nations that share its chosen identity—Islam. For 3000 years Pakistan has been in a nearly constant state of transition—resisting, submitting, and adapting to the various armies and influences that have swept through it. Its modern form is an artificial construct, established in 1947 when British India was divided into independent states for Hindus and Muslims. As a result of the hasty and often arbitrary way the borders were drawn, millions of people discovered that their ancestral homes were suddenly in the wrong nation. They became refugees in their own country, uprooted by invisible rules they did not comprehend and could not control, and told that an unfamiliar place should now be called home.

Often lost in the shuffle of history, Pakistan is a country in between, straddled between the turbulent Middle East and exotic India; between strategic location and cultural displacement. Though it is the planet's ninth most populous nation, it has often played the pawn in superpower games. In the 1950s and early 1960s, the United States had an air base in northern Pakistan, near Peshawar—part of a "mutual defense pact" that was a thinly disguised front for CIA operations. It was from here that Gary Powers's now-famous U2 spy plane took off, later to be shot down over the Soviet Union. In the aftermath of this scandal, the air base was permanently shut down. Murree Christian School benefited from the crisis, however, receiving donations of furniture and supplies from the USAF barracks, including a number of very memorable triple-deck steel-framed bunk beds.

Pakistan's rich heritage is the result of how it has adapted to its many conquerors while somehow retaining its own identity, accommodating while remaining proudly independent. At the foot of the Murree Hills, between the ancient city Taxila and the new capital Islamabad, the Soan Pebble culture developed 500,000 years ago and left behind some of the earliest artifacts of human existence anywhere in Asia. Enigmatic rock drawings indicate that Neolithic tribes in this area were studying the stars 2000 years before Stonehenge. Here, the four highest mountain ranges come together in a knot of hymn-compelling peaks known as the Roof of the World. Pakistan's Hunza valley provided the inspiration for the mythical Shangri-la of James Hilton's *Lost Horizon*, a modern fable about a place that was paradise only so long as it remained in total isolation from the outside world (a lot like the evangelical boarding school where I grew up).

In real life, monumental forces of change would come through this region, channeled between the barren hills of the Khyber Pass with its swashbuckling warriors and the pastoral beauty of Kashmir. In 500 B.C. the Persian emperor Cyrus the Great invaded the area, followed by Alexander the Great a hundred years later. Alexander never made it into India, but his final push eastward opened up trade and influence between Western civilization and the Orient for the first time. The fabled Silk Road found its midpoint in what is now northern Pakistan, where the city-state of Taxila flourished with a distinctive mingling of Roman, Greek, and Indian cultures. Its university drew philosophers, royalty, and spiritual pilgrims from both Europe and Asia. Marco Polo passed through here on his way to the courts of Kubla Khan. The "Middle Way" of Buddhism, though founded in India, achieved its greatest articulation at this crossroads, spreading religious reformation into Tibet and China.

In the sixth century A.D., while their cousin Attila was sacking Rome, the White Huns pillaged the Persian Empire, plunging India into its own Dark Ages. Then, early in the eighth century, invaders from Iraq and Syria brought much of the subcontinent under Muslim rule for almost a thousand years with various dynasties (mostly of Mongolian and Turkish descent) battling, ascending, and being overthrown. Bubar the Tiger followed Tamurlane the Earth Shaker. In 1526, Bubar took Delhi and became the first of the great Mogul emperors whose dominion would extend from the Persian border in the west to the Bay of Bengal, and from the Himalayas to the Indian Ocean. It was the richest empire the world had ever seen and it lasted just 200 years, until the British— the last foreigners to subjugate the region—began mapping the Indian subcontinent for Queen Victoria. Bubar's grandson was Akbar the Great. And his grandson was Shah Jahan, who built the Taj Mahal, as well as the Red Fort of Delhi and the Shalimar Gardens in Lahore. In the minds of many people, the architectural stamp of Islam would remain the subcontinent's most potent symbol.

* * *

THOSE of us who grew up at Murree Christian School—less than sixty miles from present-day Taxila—were neither pilgrims nor conquerors. We, too, were foreigners; yet in this narrow crucible through which so much history had funneled, we never questioned our sense of belonging. The peculiar conditions of our being there created a spiritual geography we simply called "home."

Nestled in the forested foothills of the great Himalayan mountains, Murree Christian School sits 7,500 feet above the plains in northern Pakistan—a developing country that is 98 percent Muslim. Murree is a summer town, a former colonial "hill station" of the British raj. Some students came from as far away as the United Arab Emirates, but most of our families were scattered across the plains of Pakistan—on rural mission stations or in Christian hospitals, colleges, and technical schools in larger towns or cities.

In June, when the wilting heat of the plains became almost unbearable, our parents came up to Murree from their mission stations across the country and took us out of boarding for the summer. They studied Urdu at the Murree Language School, or just rested and enjoyed the luxury of fellowship with other missionaries. And for three months we got to go to day school, like kids "back home." A real school bus came wheezing around the hill to pick us up.

With our families together, attending the big church in Murree and having dinner with other families, the summers provided the closest thing to a "normal" community. But even then we often experienced those months as "single-parent families," when our fathers were too busy to leave their work on the plains for more than a few weeks. All too soon our parents returned to their mission stations and we went back into boarding for the fall term. It wasn't possible to keep the facilities heated during the winter months, so we took our long vacation in December, January, and February.

Like nomads, we moved with the seasons. Four times a year we packed up and moved to, or back to, another temporary home. As with the seasons, each move offered something to look forward to while something had to be given up. We grew older and we came and went, not on the basis of the calendar or the school year but the weather. Each annual cycle began and ended with a ritual passage—a children's caravan called the "train party."

Fifty or sixty of us from MCS traveled together in specially designated coaches on a public train, back to our various homes "down the line." For some boys and girls, the journey lasted twenty-eight hours, spanning the length of the Indus River—from Rawalpindi, at the foot of the mountains, a thousand miles to Karachi, on the coast. After the winter break, another train party gathered us together like the Pied Piper and took us away from our families again.

We learned early that "home" was an ambiguous concept, and wherever we lived, some essential part of our lives was always someplace else. So we were always in two minds. We learned to be happy and sad at the same time. We learned to be independent and we learned that things were out of our control. We learned the reassuring familiarity of routine and the comforting exactness of being able to pack everything needed for life into a single footlocker and a bedroll. We had the security and the consolation that whenever we left one place we were returning to another, already familiar one.

"Home" might refer to the school dormitory or to the house where we stayed during the summer, to our family's home where our parents worked, or, more broadly, to the country of our citizenship. And while we might have some sense of belonging to all of these places, we felt fully at home in none of them. Boarding life seemed to have the most consistency, but there we were separated from our siblings and shared one "parent" with twenty other kids. As it grew colder we could look forward to going home for the holidays. We were always eager to be reunited with our families, but after three months of separation from our friends, we were just as eager to go back. Every time we got on the train we experienced both abandonment and communion.

So, too, in the larger cycle of furloughs—every three or four or five years, depending on the leniency or economic ability of the various mission boards: Our families went home to Canada or the States or New Zealand for awhile and then our parents left their home countries for another term abroad, and we came *home* to Pakistan. And yet, soon after we got there, we dreamed about going "home"! (Our parents shared this ambivalence: When they came home on furlough they felt like visitors, anxious to return to the place of their calling. It has been said that missionaries only feel at home on the airplane in between.)

The train party stitched together our patchwork sense of belonging until eventually, when our parents changed jobs, or there was a medical crisis in the family, or we graduated from high school, the cycles ended with crashing finality. But the ambiguity did not. For our parents, life on the mission field was an occupation; they eventually resigned or retired and become "former missionaries." But we will never be former "missionary kids"; it is our inheritance. As MKs, we grew up straddled between worlds; not fully reconciled to one or the other. Only much later would we become aware of the chasm our circumstances had created for us.

We were a curious tribe, a scrabble of diverse national origins and local circumstances, yet united by our common lot and the larger purpose that had brought us to MCS. Our families lived in isolated villages and in modern cities; as the only expatriates in the area (like mine) or in communities of other missionaries. Our parents worked with tribal people and with large institutions; they were literacy campaigners and Bible translators, technical advisors and evangelists, doctors and nurses, teachers and administrators; but mostly they saw themselves as "witnesses" to the love of Jesus, and as colleagues and friends to the Pakistanis they had come "to serve."

In the 1960s and 1970s the majority of our families were from the United States. A great number also came from England and Scotland and other Commonwealth countries, and from Germany, Sweden, Finland, and Norway as well, representing major Protestant denominations—Baptists, Presbyterians, Lutherans, Anglicans, Methodists—and a host of independent mission boards. There were no Catholic missionary children in Pakistan, for the simple reason that all the Catholic missionaries working there were priests, nuns, or members of religious orders—all requiring celibacy.

There were three other American/international schools in Pakistan, but these were all in major cities and therefore impractical for the many missionary families who lived in remote areas. This situation, together with the long tradition of expatriates on the Indian subcontinent sending their children to private schools, and the concern that we would not get adequate Christian instruction (as provided by Sunday schools back home), was the reason Murree Christian School existed.

* * *

MOST of my childhood was contained within five miles on either side of the school and the larger area of Murree town—even weekend campouts were rarely more than twenty or thirty miles away from the school. A secret garden that only rarely hinted of the primal terrors just a few miles beyond, it was still full of mystery after ten years of active exploration. It seemed an endless kingdom; only now do I realize how tiny it was.

The self-contained quality of a missionary boarding school in a foreign country made our world even smaller. MCS was an old-fashioned evangelical institution, and its often rigid social norms and standards were expressed as much in attitude and expectations as in the school rules. What saved us from the parochialness that often plagues rural religious communities in Western countries was the very foreignness that caused our isolation in the first place. The global diversity within our small world made it difficult for us to make the kind of cultural presumptions often associated with evangelical or fundamentalist groups. The British or the Norwegians, for example, didn't necessarily agree with the Americans about whether listening to jazz or rock music, playing cards, or going to the cinema were sins or not.

Although we represented fifteen different countries among us, the student population rarely exceeded 160 for all twelve grades. Another fifty adults were there as teachers and boarding staff (not counting the Pakistani servants), making up a community all told of only 210 people. My Scottish chemistry teacher was also my physical education teacher and my Sunday school teacher; my boarding "father" in junior high (a New Zealander) also taught biology. I knew everyone and their sister, or who they were married to, and both their first and last names. For ten years I attended class with essentially the same eight or nine kids; I ate breakfast, sat for "devotions," played, and did chores with a slightly larger group. Every three years we moved from the charge of one houseparent to another, but continued to relate with the same core staff. In many ways, MCS was the ultimate small town. A forty-mile trip to the nearest big city was a major expedition, visitors were a big event, and, in spite of the Christian values we so earnestly embraced, "outsiders"—new students or staff—often had difficulty fitting in. Yet for better or worse MCS was a known quantity. It was reliable.

We proudly distinguished ourselves from the "ugly Americans" in the Foreign Service and international businesses, disdaining their lives of luxury and aloofness from the "real" Pakistan. But the essential characteristics of an expatriate lifestyle— practiced by almost all Westerners living in Third World countries—are the same: privilege, status, and an artificially high standard of living (in contrast to both the local population and what could have been afforded in one's home country). We were not immune to the attitudes inevitably bred in such a situation. It was hard not to feel superior.

Our circumstances gave us a certain cross-cultural broad-mindedness, yet we were ignorant of so many things. The Pakistanis we had the most direct contact with were servants—encouraging prejudicial stereotypes about the culture in which we were guests. We had even more misconceptions about our home countries. During the sixties and seventies there were almost no Pakistani students at MCS and only one African-American boy, and he stayed for only a couple of terms. Thus, we were unaware of the racial and ethnic identifications that define much of a person's sense of belonging—and create many community tensions—even in Western nations. We were sheltered, too, from both the diversity and the divisions that characterize the expressions of Christianity. Similarly, the only professions considered worth pursuing were those that could be used in "God's work" on the mission field; we had no role models who were lawyers, artists, or philosophers. The world we grew up in seemed like a cohesive, self-evident reality. Its multiple layers and uncertainties became more apparent when we returned "home" to an unfamiliar country. And the internal contradictions built into our background made the social displacement from this transition doubly isolating.

At MCS, we took it for granted that moral issues were of central importance in every aspect of life. But "back home" this seemed to be a rare perspective, even in church; and, except in the churches that supported them, the fact that our parents were on a mission from God no longer held any special status. The defining myths of our missionary childhood inevitably lost some of their meaning when removed so completely from the context that shaped them. While the resulting dis-ease often went unacknowledged or unarticulated until much later, we had, in fact, become cultural orphans.

More than twenty years after leaving Pakistan, this legacy still haunts me. Like a ghost train chugging through my blood, it goes unnoticed for long spells, imperceptibly pushing along my pulse, only to clatter randomly through my dreams. I do not always recognize the source of this restless train inside me, but there are things that make its distant rhythm suddenly close—the smell of kerosene or pine sap, a mango's slippery taste, the sight of a Land-Rover, the curve of a wooded hillside, a social embarrassment, or the loss of a friend. Underneath the rush and rattle of life, the little engine keeps nudging me like the phantom itch of an amputated limb.

* * *

WE did not hunt lions at MCS; we were not forced to flee native rebellions or face the tides of historic changes often associated with missionary tales from Africa or China. None of us became an astronaut or a senator. None of our parents were martyred and we were only mildly inconvenienced by two short wars between Pakistan and India (in 1965, over Kashmir, and in 1971, related to the civil war in East Pakistan). The worst traumas most of us experienced were schoolyard teasings or adolescent confrontations with authority. Our daily life was dramatic—as it is for all young children. In most essential ways we lived a normal life.

So why did MCS have such a lasting impact on all those who passed through it—not just on those of us who grew up there but also on the student who spent only second and third grades there? Or the short-term missionary who served on staff at MCS for only two years and is still haunted by the experience twenty years later? What makes these memories so compelling, something more than dusty nostalgia for an obscure institution?

Perhaps the answer lies in the series of paradoxes that define the commonality of those who share a similar background:

- the simultaneously disruptive and stabilizing effect of boarding school, taking us from our families yet providing a strong, reliable community that we called home;

- the intercultural challenges *within* the insular, evangelical environment of an international and interdenominational school, and the often limited interaction we had with our host country;

- the feeling of being at home in several countries or cultures but not completely at home in any of them;

- the tension between the rich experiential education of such an upbringing, which instills a sort of global wisdom, and the loneliness that often comes with the uprooting, loss, and cultural displacement that are a part of it; and

- the conflict between our inner and outer realities—such as dealing with our memories of this experience when feelings are more real than facts yet have less authority.

The community of strangers—our experience of family with other global nomads—is one of the large and often unrecognized paradoxes of this heritage. Most of us returned to our "home" countries one by one and felt the impact of our uprooting as individuals. Yet the "unique" background that caused our sense of isolation is shared by huge numbers of people.

* * *

A recent book by William Nerin is pointedly titled *You Can't Grow Up Till You Go Back Home* (New York: Crossroad, 1993). Indeed, there are probably no questions more ancient or more compelling for the human soul than "Where did I come from?" and "Where do I belong?" Individuals, tribes, and civilizations have been preoccupied with these questions, stimulating the greater portion of art, ritual, and mythology throughout history. And they are an integral part of the more modern obsession, "Who am I?" But for missionary kids, the effort to explore our ethnic and cultural roots presents an enigma. We cannot just turn to our grandparents and say, "Where did our family come from?" because in fact our family is not the same as theirs. Our family, our homeland, is in the company of others with similar experience. Our heritage was not formed by a national tradition but by a particular situation. And when we left the artificial communities of our upbringing not only were we culturally uprooted, but so was our family tree.

In September 1990 I attended a "transition seminar" by David Pollock on TCKs and the predictable patterns that often result from growing up in a country other than the one your parents call home. It was a cathartic moment in my life—as memorable as my religious conversion at age fifteen. For the first time I didn't feel alone, I didn't have to explain myself, and I understood that there was nothing wrong with me for being who I was.

Global nomads often overlook—or deny—the accumulated grief that is also part of our heritage, partly, perhaps, because we have had no empathetic place in which to express that grief. In his seminar, David Pollock illustrated these several themes with stories that articulated deep feelings that until then I had only dimly comprehended. Many global nomads have found this "naming" of their common heritage to be both liberating and empowering. Again and again, when TCKs come to a meeting of others like themselves, their response is, "at last, I feel at home."

For many, this is enough. Such contact helps bring closure and can provide a sense of community in the present. For me, and perhaps others, this "naming" of an identifiable culture I could call my own is only a first step. I needed to rediscover the elements of my own particular heritage. The three years I spent writing about my childhood became its own story. The long, deliberate process of untangling and reconnecting the disparate threads from my past led not only to renewed friendships, but to unexpected experiences of grace. The journey took me from feeling a camaraderie with Alex Hailey doing scholarly research for *Roots* to feeling like a poster child for the "healing of memories" movement; and, finally, to a very personal quest into the meaning and purpose of community.

I wrote bluntly and in detail about situations that were still painful twenty years later. And then I tried to honestly and fairly re-create the context in which these events took place. But also an essential part of reconciliation, I found, was "overwriting" old feelings with new experiences. For me, this process culminated in a year-long dialogue with my father through journal-writing and correspondence, inspired and structured by Frederick Buechner's book of daily meditations, *Listening to Your Life*. The intimate sharing and empathy brought forth by this exercise would have been unimaginable to either of us even a few years earlier.

Seeking a deeper understanding of where I've come from led inevitably, as I see in retrospect, to a greater understanding of those who shaped me. I remember a particular telephone conversation and hearing the quake of old age in the voice of a teacher who I felt had deeply wronged me in ninth grade. Years of research, therapy, and prayer—none of these changed my perspective so much as that one moment. I finally have become free from the emotional weight of childhood memories—the hurts incurred by parents and peers and the powerlessness produced by the boarding school experience. Time, I have learned, is three-dimensional, not linear, and I now have a meaningful place within the community of those who share my past.

My desire for reliable, *accessible* friendships and a cohesive sense of place in the present is, of course, still far from satisfied. But I have come much closer to finding a sense of home within myself.

Notes

1. I am indebted to Stephen Neill, *A History of Christian Missions* (New York: Penguin, 1986), for some of these statistics.

You Can't
Go "Home" Again
Kay Branaman Eakin

KAY BRANAMAN EAKIN *began her research on TCKs after her family's evacuation from Addis Ababa in 1977. Many of her key findings are included in* The Foreign Service Teenager—at Home in the U.S.: A Few Thoughts for Parents Returning with Teenagers. *She has served as an advisor to* Around the World in a Lifetime (AWAL), *a social organization for Foreign Service teens, and is president of the Board of the Foreign Service Youth Foundation. She has conducted reentry and transition training both in the United States and abroad, and has assisted in the writing and production of videotapes on issues related to raising children abroad.*

WHEN I FIRST READ Thomas Wolfe's *You Can't Go Home Again*, I was in my twenties and little-traveled. I knew almost nothing about the effects of mobility on adults, let alone on children or teenagers, but Wolfe convinced me that returning home would be a difficult proposition. Now, years later, I have experienced many moves and returned "home" on several occasions. I survived. I realize that I am changed by my experiences and that "home" has also changed, although somewhat less than I. Still, every time, after a few months back I have reattached and reintegrated into my own culture. What has changed, more than anything else, are my perceptions of "home." But I have made those moves as an adult, and I am increasingly convinced that this has made all the difference.

My children, who began moving within the first year or two of their lives, don't have the same perception of what "home" is; in many ways, now that they are in their thirties, they still have not really "come home again." Their ideas of "home" are different from mine. Before I was twenty-one, I had only two homes, one until I was eight and the other until I married. Each of my children first moved abroad at age four or younger. Each of them has lived in five or more countries and in six different states within the United States. And although each of them returned here to live, more or less permanently, between the ages of fourteen and nineteen, none felt that he was returning home.

Along the way, each of them has become a third culture kid (TCK). David Pollock defines the term as follows: "A TCK is an individual who, having spent a significant part of the developmental years in a culture other than the parents' culture, develops a sense of relationship to all of those cultures while not having full ownership in any."[1] This phenomenon goes by many names, including multiculture kids (MCKs) and, more specifically, missionary kids (MK), overseas brats (U.S. military), and global nomads, the term most commonly used for adult TCKs. In her book of the same name, Carolyn Smith uses the term "absentee Americans" for those who have returned to the United States to live. Whichever term is used, the sense of home will be forever different for them than it was for me or for someone growing up in one country. Home, after all, is the place where you feel at home. Pollock tells the possibly apocryphal story about children going to visit their grandmother in the States and being greeted by, "Aren't you glad to be home?" and not being able to reply, "No, it may be my parents' home, but it's not my home."

Ursula Lindsey writes in *Notes from a Traveling Childhood*, "Physically, I am here. But everything that belongs to me, everything that defines me, is on the other side of the Atlantic Ocean."² Young people who grow up in another culture may carry a U.S. passport and may ultimately settle in the United States, but rarely, if ever, does this country become home to them in the same way that it does for those of us who grew up here before embarking on a nomadic lifestyle.

My own experience as a nomadic adult and my interest in the effects of reentry, particularly upon teenagers, started with my own family's moves around the world. At that time very little had been written about what happens to mobile youth in transition and upon reentry. A graduate course in adolescent psychology led me to write a research paper on the topic of teen reentry, followed by more writing in the late 1970s and 1980s; since then I have observed and continued to describe its effects, mostly anecdotally. While there has been more research in recent years, there is still a paucity of published materials. There has, however, been an interesting occurrence; Carolyn Smith, in researching repatriates' perspectives on America, and Ruth and John Useem, Kathleen Finn Jordan, and Ann Baker Cottrell, in researching adult TCK attitudes, had an overwhelming response, not just to the written questionnaire but with penciled-in personal responses. Obviously, those adult TCKs are anxious to talk about and share their experiences.

I first traveled abroad with my family in the U.S. Foreign Service, and my first observations of the phenomenon of reentry were among our friends who came and went from foreign postings. As we continued to travel and meet military, business, and missionary families, I noticed that their reactions to these moves were, if not identical, at least quite similar. In addition, as I met other foreign nationals living outside their own country, I noticed that their children had similar reactions. It didn't matter if it was a Dane or a Japanese or an Italian or a Swazi—these children had difficulty adjusting to a move "home." (For many of those who have lived in America, this transition has been particularly thorny when moving from the United States to their home country.) Their experience of living in another cultural environment has changed forever the perception of home carried by someone who grows up uniculturally.

G. Molloy, writing in *Liaison*, states that

> the return to Ottawa after a series of postings was the most difficult adjustment for our older children.... When these "third culture kids" return home they must confront the reality that they are not as Canadian as they thought, and they are strangers in their own land.[3]

Stefan Hormuth's study of the diplomatic community in Germany,[4] Hiroshi Iwama's research on returnees in Japan,[5] and Barbro Hall and Gunnila Masreliez-Steen's survey of Swedish Foreign Service children[6] also indicated that the return "home" was not easy on those Germans and Japanese and Swedes who had spent part of their childhood abroad. A Colgate University administrator commented on an American TCK who was having problems adapting to his U.S. experience: "He looks like an American, he talks like an American, but he's really more like a foreign student."[7]

Interestingly, these Japanese, Danish, Italian, Swazi, and American TCKs often have far more in common with each other than they do with the peer group of their own individual countries. The commonality of the TCK experience, of the differences they share based on those experiences, is often what draws them together. In many instances, the sense and pull of these differences seems to become stronger as TCKs grow older.

A friend in her early thirties, whom I've known since she was fourteen, spoke of her new acceptance of what her TCK identity now meant to her. Exposed to support groups for returning TCKs as a teenager and younger adult, she was only marginally comfortable with that label and identity. She recently met a coworker who is a TCK and active in Global Nomads International, and she plans on getting involved, too. "I know I'm really ready to think about all those things now," she confided.

> I just returned from a month with my parents in Africa, and I'm looking forward to being able to talk to other Global Nomads. They'll understand about my experiences, and I'll be able to share with them what it means to have had this kind of life.

Reentry is not an easy experience for anyone—adult, child, or teen. Most of us who have done it know that the hardest move is often the return to one's home country. Cross-cultural research indicates that reentry can be more difficult and take a longer adjustment period than initial entry into the overseas setting. As I meet with parents during that crucial first year home, I often hear them lament the same losses as their children. In fact, some research indicates that those who adapt best to a foreign environment often have the most difficulty returning to their own country. But adults often have a stronger idea of what they left at home, and while the return may be inconvenient and the lifestyle might not be nearly as attractive or exciting, they usually had a unicultural experience during their developmental years and, as I did, eventually readapt into their own culture.

Teenagers seem to have the most difficulty dealing with reentry, although, being teenagers, part of it may be that they are more articulate or more forceful with attention-getting behavior. However, I have watched children as young as five mourn their losses, particularly the loss of caretakers. At that age "home" is the place they remember leaving, not the place to which they returned and of which they may have no conscious memory.

The sense of loss of friends, of place, of familiarity is one that many TCKs carry throughout their lives. Betsy, a middle-aged woman, speaking of growing up in China, reminisced,

> Once I knew a charm to bring a snail out of its shell, but it was in a language I no longer know in a country I shall never live in again.... There was an unalterable otherness that comes from being raised in a very different time and place, perhaps one that had made [me] a perpetual traveler.... I shall always know ... that the bridge of my nose is too high.[8]

Children raised overseas are changed by their experiences abroad. Being a parent to these mobile children often requires more commitment rather than less, particularly in transition times and especially in reentry. If this is true, what can families do to ameliorate the effects of the moves? What can communities (of military, missionary, business, or diplomats) or their sponsoring agencies or companies do to ease the return "home"? Most important, what can teenagers do to make this often painful move one that provides positive personal growth?

Before we can answer those questions, we need to know what the particular issues are for young people returning to their "home" culture. While society often undergoes many changes during an absence (one need only look at the increased sexuality, violence, and drugs that are commonly examined in detail and often glamorized in the mass media), I have worked with reentering teens over the last twenty years and have observed that many of the core issues haven't really changed. No matter what the sponsor or the reason for the overseas sojourn, most teens are made to feel that they are representatives of their country. In an overseas expatriate or host national environment, they are known as "Americans" (or Danes, Japanese, Italians, or Nigerians). Imagine their surprise, then, when they return "home" and don't feel that they have much in common with their contemporaries.

While the increased immediacy of communication today (CNN, for example) and the worldwide distribution of music videos and movies give many teenagers more opportunity to follow the "in" scene at "home," what's "in" today is often "out" pretty quickly and what's "in" may vary according to the particular crowd. Trying to figure out those cues is not easy when your heart and mind are still in Valletta, Bangkok, or Accra. These young people have often been quite competent when dealing with their peers abroad, and, because of opportunities to interact with adults overseas, they are often more assured and comfortable than other teens when dealing with adults. Unfortunately, this skill with adults rarely translates into fitting in well with their "home" peer group. This lack of peer collaboration perpetuates their dependence on parents, again delaying the teens' developmental progress in moving on to become an independent adult.

When families return "home," family members often become even closer, providing needed support for teenagers who are struggling to develop new friendships once again. What happens, though, is that the teenager's independence is, once more, delayed. The reentering teens are trying to fit into a peer system where many of their compatriots are leading what seems to be a life highly independent of their parents. If teens try to mimic the pattern they see in the local culture, parents often are uncertain how to respond. Concerned that their child not make a wrong choice, they often tighten control over their son's or daughter's activities, thus preventing their teen from taking the necessary developmental steps toward independence.

One problem these mobile youth seem to carry with them is the habit of leaving problems behind rather than dealing with them. Someone who lives in one community and attends one school cluster learns, of necessity, problem-solving skills in dealing with interpersonal relationships. Because they often move on before resolving any disagreements they may have had with friends or teachers, these young people learn to avoid dealing with problems. They can move on, yet they carry with them the baggage of unresolved relationships.

Perhaps the problems that are of most concern, especially to parents, are drugs, alcohol, and sex. These problems are particularly troublesome for parents when they are unable to be around after school to discuss or monitor their teenagers' activities. Returning "home" is often an expensive proposition for families who may have had housing costs and other expenses provided for by their overseas sponsor. At a time when many returning young people need a great deal of support and advice, their parents must become involved in their jobs shortly after they arrive. Even when parents are available at the end of the school day, the lines of communication may not be open and both children and parents may not feel comfortable discussing these topics. In the position of trying to decide what rules to enforce in a community without the parameters and mores to which they have become accustomed in overseas communities, parents sometimes tend to become overly protective of their teens—or abdicate their role.

At the same time, in order to find attention and nurturance, young people often turn to inappropriate peers to provide the counsel and attention that parents working long hours and commuting long distances are not providing. Counselors in the Washington, D.C., area, for example, speak of kids bringing up kids, becoming inappropriate counselors to each other. This is a situation that teens themselves see as something they'd like to change. Many returning teens say they would like to spend more time in family activities, as they often did when abroad. What they really want are guidelines. While it may seem to parents that children want guidelines only to have something to rebel against, for many these guidelines provide protection. Teens may complain and argue about them, but rules give them an explanation or excuse when peers suggest involvement in drugs or other activities they wish to avoid.

Families have often felt that an overseas assignment protected their teenagers by keeping them overseas in what they saw as a safer environment. The results of a survey of teens in twelve American/international overseas high schools in the early

1900s, however, belie that assumption. While the survey, conducted by a State Department doctor, may provide a modicum of relief to parents about their concerns of bringing children back to a changed society, the downside is that overseas life is not as protective as some parents would like to believe. The survey questioned expatriate teens about their use of alcohol, tobacco, and drugs; their participation in sexual activity; and their experience with violence. Their replies were much like those of their counterparts at home in terms of risky behaviors. Areas of significant statistical difference included fewer sexual experiences (but more medical treatment for sexually transmitted diseases), less lifetime use of alcohol, minimally less use of marijuana and much less use of cocaine, and less cigarette smoking in grades 9 and 10. Actual suicide attempts, disturbingly, were higher among overseas American students than among their U.S.-based counterparts.

Students have a range of good and bad experiences attending schools abroad (as they do in their home countries), but overseas schools are often smaller, with fewer students per class, and often encompass grades K-12. In this transient environment, there is usually an acceptance, even a true welcoming, of newcomers, an opportunity to be a big fish in a little pond—and the school is often supported by a cohesive, concerned community. Returning to a U.S. public school environment is often daunting; at a minimum, it is not easy.

The student returning to the United States finds that many school teams, at least for fall sports, are usually chosen and have even practiced before the school year actually begins. Academic requirements may vary; Virginia, for example, has a Virginia history graduation requirement, which is usually fulfilled as an underclassman. If a student arrives as a senior and doesn't know about the requirement, enrollment counselors don't always catch the omission. Since many students have been classmates since grade school, social groups and cliques are often fully established. Teachers are sometimes well-intentioned and even knowledgeable about the different backgrounds expatriate students bring to the classroom, but as one student observed, "It's really a bummer when it's only the teachers who talk to you."

Many reentering teenagers feel that they have no control over their lives. Often happy overseas, or at least as happy as most teenagers are willing to admit, they are suddenly uprooted by a parent's reassignment and whisked away "home." This phenomenon, which may have occurred several times in their lives, suddenly becomes an issue for the evolving young adult. By the time these same youngsters are teenagers returning "home," and particularly if they have experienced several moves, the sense of loss lasts longer and is more painful. They have either left or been left by all their friends. Teenagers, after all, are going through the most turbulent physical and emotional changes of their lives, that of moving from childhood to puberty, from a time in which their family is most important to them to a time when what their friends say and think is far more important. When their adolescent changes are compounded by a move away from their peer support system, they often react quite strongly or, even worse, withdraw into their own world supported by "their" music, which speaks to them but usually not to their parents. The difficulty in finding a new peer group exacerbates their sense of a lack of control over what happens to them. When this move is also accompanied by a family breakup, the effect on the teen is doubly hard. The feeling of being an outsider or an observer is often mentioned by these returnees. One adult TCK talks about the advantage of living in Washington, D.C.: He can continue his lifetime experience as an outsider watching other people be the actors in a city where he feels that he can't find a meaningful leadership role. Here he can continue to be the ultimate observer.

One of the challenges that a reentering teenager faces is that of finding good friends, or even one good friend. Julia Love, writing in *Notes from a Traveling Childhood*, says, "In Europe I was 'the American,' but in my own country I felt like a foreigner."[10]

Often these young people, as a means of protection, have started to withdraw from the whole process of making new friends in order to be protected against the hurt of losing yet another friend. This difficulty in finding a comfortable peer group often causes teenagers who have spent a couple of years back in the States to look forward eagerly to heading abroad again. They are anxious to repeat the overseas experience because they feel that they aren't really leaving any friends behind in their U.S. high school. This is in real contrast to the way most of them speak about their overseas friendship experiences. Interestingly enough, though, once they have established themselves in the States they often want to finish their high school experience without another move. Having finally settled into a U.S. high school, they often express a desire to finish high school without a move and not have to go though the process yet again.

Families need to maintain both short-and long-term strategies for helping their children make all their moves and, especially, the important transition to reentry. As children grow up overseas, they need to be encouraged to keep in touch with friends and family they have left behind. A trip back to the country of origin may be more important for children and their ultimate adjustment to "home" than their parents' dream of a European vacation. For teenagers it may be important to have an opportunity to return "home" and attend driving school and get a driver's license. Exposing children to a wide assortment of activities and sports may also make moving around and returning home easier. It is often possible overseas to be able to participate and get lessons in sports much more easily and reasonably than at home. Each skill a child develops may provide another opportunity or opening to a small group, something that comes in handy following a move. One pair of brothers has used the field hockey skill first learned at their English boarding school to play in and referee field hockey matches both in the United States and internationally. The international field hockey friends they made upon their reentry twenty years ago as beginning college students remain their closest friends today.

One of the long-term strategies that can help children make the ultimate move of returning to their passport country is planning a child's education in advance. Making a conscious decision to allow a child to stay in the same educational system throughout the school career may be more helpful in the long run than a two-year stint in the local French-speaking school. However, if a child has a particular gift for language and might be able to continue in that national system, it may be the right answer. Extending a tour to accommodate a senior year or to give three or four years of continuous school experience is often advised. It is worth noting that there are some indications that children who attend boarding high schools in the United States during parents' overseas postings sometimes have an easier time adapting to the States as "home."

There was a time when the ideal for many expatriate families was to keep a "stiff upper lip." Times have changed, and many societies now encourage at least a minimal show of emotions and feelings. It is important that children realize that parents have feelings and concerns, too, and that the choices that must be made are as painful for parents as for them. Ruth E. Van Reken, in her book *Letters Never Sent,* tells of returning to boarding school as a child, thinking her parents didn't miss her when she was away, until the day she looked out the window of the small plane returning her to school to see her mother in tears and being comforted by her father.

One long-term strategy used by many expatriate families abroad has been to work to develop support services in their communities. Exemplary organizations now exist in such far-flung cities as Kuala Lumpur, Singapore, Cairo, and Taipei, several of which were originally organized and staffed by Joel Wallach and Gail A. Metcalf. This couple suggests that families meet with other parents to establish clear community guidelines for their children that are appropriate to the local environment, attend parent workshops and seminars, and organize healthy, supervised teen activities.[12]

Frequent communication with family and friends is important, through whatever means is within the family's financial capacity, including letters, e-mail, audio- and videotapes, and long-distance calls. Any or all can help teenagers keep friendships intact throughout the overseas experience. The Write Connection Program,[13] or similar programs that help establish a writing habit, can be helpful, particularly for younger children.

But now the time has come to return home— the time for short-term and long-term strategies has passed. How, then, do families go about handling an impending move? How can they help their children and teenage returnees continue their personal growth and development while preserving their very special cultural knowledge?

In order to make a successful reentry, attention must be paid not only to a successful adjustment at home, but to a good leave-taking of the country of assignment. Closure must be put on the overseas sojourn. Parents need to provide opportunities for their children to say proper goodbyes to the post and to their friends. While organizing formal ways of doing that may be easier with preteens, some teenagers will accept an offer of a farewell party, and all can be encouraged to do their leave-taking less formally. This may be a harder task, however, if a child has already started withdrawing from close relationships.

Many overseas communities and schools run reentry or transition programs at the end of the academic year. These programs provide children with the opportunity to talk about the move and how they feel about it. They must know that they have permission to express their unhappiness at the impending move. It is helpful if they realize that their parents and their siblings are also ambivalent about moving. Discussions about what life will be like for everyone in the family upon return may elicit some open sharing of concerns and apprehensions among all the family members. Some families have found that treating the move home as a move to another post can ease the transition. It can be helpful to make plans as a family about tourist attractions to check out upon arrival "home," taking advantage of cultural and social opportunities as they would at any new posting. If a family anticipates the logistics as being particularly difficult or fears that it may take a long time to find a place to live, it may be helpful to arrange summer camp activities for returning teens and children.

It used to be possible to put strong closure on the overseas experience by taking a leisurely ship voyage during which the family could focus on the country they had just left and talk fondly about their experiences there. Unfortunately, this is almost entirely a thing of the past. Modern travel permits us to fly home supersonically after a rushed farewell period. Families arrive "home" very quickly, often within hours of departure, and plunge directly into reestablishing their home. A more ideal way of re-entry, sometimes also saving time and nerves, can be accomplished by spending a short time at a quiet resort or even a weekend in an unknown city (in which there are no family or friends to be visited) before beginning these tasks. Taking time out in this way can pave the way for a more relaxing and calm transition and provides an opportunity to talk about the impending arrival.

We all have a tendency to "improve" on the last country we lived in once we have gone. This is particularly true when we return home, especially when home doesn't live up to our idealized expectations. Teenagers, in particular, often belittle what they find when they come "home." The culture shock of the move for teenagers can be compared to a roller-coaster ride—initial excitement followed by down times, occasional pockets of excitement and then down again (when they're sure they'll never fit in). They are often angry at their parents for moving them but may not feel comfortable expressing that anger. Like most unexpressed anger, it often comes out unexpectedly at inappropriate times. Younger siblings may be making a quicker adjustment, which often makes teens feel that there is something wrong with them.

Support from parents is one of the strongest indicators that mobile children will develop a sense of mastery of their environment after a move. Such support enables children to handle all moves more easily, particularly if their mother handles it well. Julius Segal, who studied and wrote extensively on resiliency in children, commented that "approaches youngsters take to life's difficulties often mirror those of the mother."[14] Segal's point was reinforced by a U.S. State Department study that indicated that "the mother has a lot of influence in how the kids adjust psychologically."[15]

Dr. Elmore Rigamer, director of medical services at the State Department, reported that one of the findings from interviews of thirty-eight Foreign Service families was that

> Boys and girls who are allowed in the family to fully express their feelings—their concerns about moving, about leaving friends behind, about where they're going—these kids end up making a better adjustment. It's important for them to let all their feelings come out without their parents interrupting them with...reassurances.[16]

Each member of the family needs a safe environment where opinions about problems of dealing with their "home" culture can be expressed. As Rigamer points out, reentry is a time when the entire family needs to feel free to talk honestly about each member's frustrations.

It is important that human resource departments in sponsoring companies and organizations provide not only predeparture counseling and workshops but also similar support for personnel and families returning to their "homes." This support needs to provide an accepting environment that allows TCKs (and their parents) to deal with the relocation process and provides models for coping with the transition.

Any experience that is enough out of the ordinary to require serious advance planning, training, and orientation is worth an opportunity for debriefing. Col. William Klein, former chief of child psychiatry at the Walter Reed Medical Center, pointed out the need for orientation seminars for military families. "Now," he said resignedly, "it's assumed you'll work it out."[17]

Guidelines for developing a returnee support system can be obtained from organizations that already have programs in operation. For example, for many years the missionary community has provided strong support through Mu Kappa (Missionary Kids/MK) and other reentry programs such as Interaction, Inc. Recent impetus has come from the results of research conducted by the MK Consultation and Resource Team/Committee on Research and Endowment. Another model is the program supported by the Foreign Service Youth Foundation, organized in 1989 as an umbrella organization to provide services for those who grow up in diplomatic families abroad. The foundation has developed a "flow of care" to assist mobile young people that includes preparation for going overseas, programs at post (including electronic dialogues with teens in the States), teen-produced videos of overseas posts, annual community service volunteer awards, publication of books such as *Notes from a Traveling Childhood*, and reentry programming. Reentry activities include workshops; welcome folders and phone calls; the organization Around the World in a Lifetime (AWAL), which organizes social and workshop-type experiences for its members; a teen-produced monthly newsletter, *Wings of AWAL*, distributed to over 250 families in the U.S. and abroad; and various other social and educational programs.

In 1995, after discovering a copy at his medical clinic, an adult TCK wrote to the *Wings of AWAL* newsletter editor: "I did not have someone that I could relate to when I got hit by the culture shock when I came from a school of 125 students into a high school of over 2,500. I do not want anyone else to go through what I did, and I think you are doing a great job by helping those cope with the changes that await them."

If the overseas personnel staff in a corporation is too small for a reentry program to be provided in-house, there are consultants scattered around the world who can develop and present a program. If this is not a viable option, community reentry activities may be available. Colleges and universities may have chapters of Global Nomads International that can provide a list of TCK reentry support programs. Local school systems may have programs that assist new students entering from overseas.

While older children have more difficulty adjusting socially upon reentry, younger children seem to have more difficulty adjusting academically while they are still developing basic reading, writing, and math skills. For less able students, mobility is an additional stress factor that can result in lower achievement. School programs should be examined closely to see which are really most appropriate for children. Once children are enrolled, parents may want to play an active role in helping their children's teachers and administrators understand the transition their youngsters are going through in returning to a home that is not really their home.

Families who seem to be most successful in helping their children reenter usually do some planning for their return "home." Advance thought goes into how to "reattach," what community resources and activities to seek out, and what churches or other community activities to return to. Research has indicated that the strongest source of support during a child's move is actively participating in planning one's new room! A family returning to "headquarters" may be able to hook up with other families that have have done so, in which there may be children who "speak the same language." Some of the most successful social gatherings in the months after return are those involving other families who have returned from the same post. Children can reestablish friendships, exchange phone numbers, and at least have long telephone talks with someone who understands *mariachis* or *samalvita*.

Part of the problem in making new friendships, of course, is finding friends with whom one has something in common. Unicultural students may not understand what it's like to live in Chiang Mai; they may not even know what part of the world, let alone in what country, Chiang Mai is located. Students who are able to hook up with other TCKs, even those who don't know where Chiang Mai is, find others who understand the lifestyle. They can share tales with peers who are accepting and are themselves anxious to find someone to talk to about their experiences. If there is no one in the community with the expatriate experience, reentering students often hook up with international students as their first contacts.

It is important for each member of the family to have a little breathing space, despite the time and assistance that family members need to give each other. Too much togetherness can exacerbate frustrations. Teenagers especially need some private time so that they can begin to feel independent. This is sometimes hard for parents to provide as they look around at what they may see as a menacing society. Encouraging teens to get involved in organized activities with other teens and an appropriate adult presence can often bring relief.

How long does it take? It varies from one person to another. Some teenagers adapt fairly quickly and find a comfortable niche in high school or college. Some even decide that they don't want to go overseas again or even to move ever again; they put down strong roots. Others take a much longer time, even years, to come to terms with the United States as home, and some never do so completely. However, most settle in pretty well during the first six months to a year. While adults realize that things will be better six months down the road, most teenagers often have not yet learned that waiting six months is acceptable. Willingness to delay gratification, to be invulnerable to social stigma and negative labels, is often difficult for teens who are still seeking their identity.

Parents sometimes err in thinking that these problems can be handled at home and put off seeking help. It may become necessary for teenagers to get professional counseling to assist them through this rocky time. When looking for a professional to assist a third culture kid, it is helpful to find someone who has some knowledge of the mobile lifestyle.

When discussing reentry, there is always a danger of stressing the pitfalls, the negative aspects of the move and of the lifestyle. The important thing for both parents and teens to remember is that most children ultimately make the transition from "there" to "here," and most even begin to think of the United States as home—not in the same way as their unicultural parents do, but in their own TCK way.

Interestingly enough, even those teens who have had
the most difficult adjustments eventually say that
they wouldn't have wanted to live any other way,
that what they learned from the overseas experience is something they wouldn't consider changing.
And most of them grow up to be responsible, contributing, interesting, and happy adults. In fact,
people often comment on their poise, resourceful-
ness, and resilience.

There are many advantages for young people
who have had the opportunity to grow up in many
cultures. As nations throughout the world become
increasingly interrelated, these are the young people
who have already learned how to observe different
societies for cues on how to interact, who often have
already learned a foreign language, perhaps even
one that isn't a "world language," and, in any case,
have learned a kind of international body language
that allows them to communicate nonverbally. The
experience of integrating into another culture and
returning to their own has equipped them with leave-
taking and other social skills, and, to a person, they
have acquired a view of the world that differs from
that of people who grow up in one culture. As one
returnee remarked,

> Global nomads have a unique perspective of
> the world, and although we are perceived as
> different, we have a great source of knowl-
> edge and information derived from experiences
> that others will grow to envy. Those who have
> lived abroad need to understand the advan-
> tages of experiencing such a change and har-
> ness that power for years to come.

Many of these young people go on to lives of
service, often overseas or with an organization with

an international element. They become the international bankers, development officers, business developers, diplomats, and representatives of international organizations. It is important for each of them to be made aware of just how valuable their growing-up experience was yesterday, is today, and will be tomorrow. Anora Sutherland, herself a global nomad and the daughter and sister of other global nomads, put it succinctly when she said, "With support, TCKs have an opportunity for the best that education has to offer—experience and confidence in handling change."

It is the responsibility of those of us who strive to provide support for this very special group of TCK youth to be sure that they get the message that the skills they have prepare them uniquely for handling change in a world with a growing international interdependency—the world of the twenty-first century.

Notes

1. David C. Pollock, Interaction, Inc., 1988.

2. Ursula Lindsey, "Nostalgia," *Notes from a Traveling Childhood* (Foreign Service Youth Foundation, Washington, D.C., 1994), p. 55.

3. G. Molloy, letter, in *Liaison*, published by the Department of External Affairs Posting Services Centre, Ottawa, Canada, 1993.

4. Stefan E. Hormuth, "Psychological Effects of Geographic Mobility on Adolescents," unpublished study results of West German Foreign Office adolescents, circa 1989. The study involved interviews with 25 families, questionnaires from families representing 189 adolescents, and a comparison group of German civil service nonmobile families.

5. Hiroshi F. Iwama, paper delivered at Conference of Internationally Mobile Children in the Third Culture Context, March 17, 1989, University of Florida.

6. Barbro Hall and Gunnila Masreliez-Steen, "The Surroundings and Development of Foreign Service Children," *Kontura Personal*, Swedish Government, Stockholm, 1982.

7. Kathleen Ambrogi, "At Home Without a Home TCKs Speak Out," *NewsLinks*, March 1992, XI:4, p. 8.

8. Stephen Bodio, *Querencia* (Livingston, Mont.: Clark City Press), p. 120.

9. Thomas A. Rodgers, M.D., "Here Are Findings of a Survey on How American Teens Behave Overseas," *State*, October 1993, pp. 20–23.

10. Julia Love, "Growing Up Internationally Mobile," *Notes from a Traveling Childhood* (Foreign Service Youth Foundation, Washington, D.C., 1994), p. 84.

11. Ruth E. Van Reken, *Letters Never Sent.* (Oakbrook, Ill.: Darwill, 1984).

12. Joel Wallach and Gail A. Metcalf, "Safe Kids, Involved Parents," *Notes from a Traveling Childhood* (Foreign Service Youth Foundation, 1994), pp. 92–104.

13. The Write Connection Program, Positive Parenting, 1-800-334-3143.

14. Julius Segal, *Parents* magazine, April, 1988.

15. Peter Steinglass and Martha E. Edwards, "Family Relocation Study: Final Report" (New York: Ackerman Institute for Family Therapy for the U.S. Department of State, 1993).

16. Elmore Rigamer, "Surprise for Mom and Dad," *State*, September 1993, p. 5.

17. Jane Friedman, "Bringing Kids Home After Living Abroad," *Washington Post*, September 18, 1990.

Religious
Culture Shock
Ruth E. Van Reken

*RUTH E. VAN REKEN is a sandwich generation TCK.
From birth until her return to the United States at age
thirteen, she lived in Kano, Nigeria. Her American father
was born and raised in Iran, and her three daughters
thrived for nine years of their childhood in Liberia. A
personal exploration of how the cycles of separation and
loss that marked her childhood had influenced her own
life led to the publication of her book,* Letters Never Sent.
*Her other publications range from Bible study guides to
articles on various topics, including "Healing the
Wounded Among Adult MKs."*

I KNEW SOMETHING WAS different when I saw
the lipstick.

"Mommy, is Aunt Susie a *Christian?*" I asked
in a horrified whisper while following my parents
down the gangplank from the *S.S. Nieuw Amsterdam*
to the firm cement of the New York pier.

My mother continued smiling and waving at
the woman who waved so energetically back at us
from that sea of welcoming faces below.

"Of course she is," Mom replied from the
side of her mouth. Her eyes remained fixed ahead
with the smile still in place. "Why on earth are
you asking?"

"But, Mom,…" I struggled to keep from getting separated as our fellow passengers pushed past us, also trying to hasten reunions with waiting relatives. "Look at her. She's got bright red lipstick on and she's wearing dangly earrings. She *couldn't* be a Christian. Christians don't do those things."

And thus, for me as an eight-year-old missionary kid, the religious culture shock of returning "home" began.

In addition to the common challenges virtually all third culture kids deal with when they enter, or reenter, their home countries, some TCKs also face additional challenges specifically related to their role as *missionary* kids. While my particular example of religious culture shock may seem extreme in these waning days of the twentieth century, most MKs can cite a similar moment. It is when they first realize that the way fellow believers in their home country express faith appears radically different from customs they've always known.

To properly understand these and other challenges specific to the reentering missionary TCK, we must first look at the missionary community itself. Paradoxically, many of the religious reentry challenges are the flip side of some of the greatest blessings MKs may experience in that community. Faith wouldn't seem so shallow at home if they hadn't seen it so powerfully lived out by missionaries all around them. On the other hand, some challenges arise from the particular idiosyncracies of any given group of missionaries. I wouldn't have worried about lipstick and earrings if those around me hadn't condemned them. So what are some of the characteristics of the missionary "third culture"?

For some people, the very word *missionary* is anathema. "How can *anyone* try to convince another person what to believe? That's terrible." And missions and missionaries are summarily dismissed with no further attempt to understand who they are, what their world is like, or even what drives them to do what they do.

For me, *missionary* is a word and a world that are part of my very identity. Its impact on me began years before my birth. "Resht, Iran" was entered in the space for "Place of Birth" on my father's passport. Yet his passport proudly proclaimed "The United States of America" across its green cover. In that same space for declaring birthplace, my American passport reads "Kano, Nigeria," while my daughter's boldly states "Monrovia, Liberia." I have cousins who were born in Kuwait, Ethiopia, Nigeria, Iran, and Sudan. A great-aunt spent three years in a Japanese internment camp after forty years as a missionary in China. Whether these members of my family were teachers, doctors, nurses, administrators, or preachers, all have been involved in mission work of some kind. This missionary world is the cocoon from which the very shape of my life has emerged.

I, and countless other adult missionary kids, grew up in perhaps the epitome of what John and Ruth Hill Useem meant when they coined the term "third culture"—the world expatriates develop that is rooted in the home culture, lived out in the host culture, but, in the end, neither fully one nor the other. It has developed a life and system of its own. The Useems called this an "interstitial culture"—a world between worlds.[1]

As a child, my specific third culture community of missionary expatriates defined its physical borders by the trim privet hedges growing in careful rows around the perimeters of our mission station. Within those friendly confines, we lived in houses made from sun-dried mud bricks that had been plastered with cement and covered with galvanized tin roofs. Each house fell into careful conformity with the next one: yellow walls, dark green trim. One after another, these buildings popped up across the landscape of our station, yellow and green monuments standing sturdily among the nim, flame-of-the-forest, and frangi-pangi trees scattered across the usually dry, barren, brown earth.

Each path connecting our look-alike houses had whitewashed stones lining its sides so we could find our way home even on the darkest nights. Carefully watered hibiscus bushes, zinnias, and morning-glories bloomed around each house, creating the only distinctions between one house and the next. All non-parental adults in the community were my "aunties" and "uncles," and their children were my friends, all closer than the cousins in the States whom I barely remembered.

Ironically, ours wasn't the only mission compound that looked like this. Throughout the country, we knew we'd found "us" when that yellow house with dark green trim began to rise up over the horizon as we drove down a rutty road to a remote station.

Reflecting on the orderliness of my childhood world now, it seems rather quaint, even a little silly. But that's one of the paradoxes. Undoubtedly, the degree of uniformity in our mission stifled the creative side of some of its members and most likely increased our culture shock when we returned to a wider world at home. On the other hand, that very uniformity and orderliness gave me a deep sense of security and belonging throughout my childhood. There were some things you could always count on. It felt familiar and safe—like the feeling I had during the short rainy seasons when I curled up under my covers, listening to the staccato of the raindrops beating on our tin roof as I fell asleep. No matter the storm, I was inside and protected.

Unlike many other TCKs who have moved from pillar to post at least every two years throughout their lives, I basically lived in one city among the same group of people from birth until I made my permanent return to the States at age thirteen. This gave me a strong sense of "home" even during the two years I went away to boarding school. Each furlough left me anxious to go home—meaning Nigeria. This type of stability in an overseas post is likely much more common for missionary kids than for TCKs from the Foreign Service or military sponsorships. Historically, missionaries went overseas and settled in a particular place for life. The idea of living in a community isn't something I can only imagine. I've done it. The mission system was my extended family in every way. I knew my tribe and where I fit in it.

No culture, however, has external uniformity alone. To be a functioning community, a group must also share deeper values and belief systems. Every culture develops its customs and mores based on that underlying value system. For example, in her book *Military Brats*, Mary Edwards Wertsch demonstrates clearly the "warrior mentality" underlying many of the social norms for those in the military subcultures.[2] Contrary to modern opinion, there is no such thing as a value-free culture. Ultimately, the only question among any group of people is, "Whose values or principles will shape this culture's expression?"

A missionary community is no different in this respect from any other. The only difference is that the values and beliefs that drive a missionary community are perhaps more objectively defined than in a secular one. The values that drive the mores of a nonmissionary group may be equally powerful, but so poorly defined that they go unnoticed. The religious community has its creeds, doctrines, and principles by which its members are to live, all clearly laid out. "Thou shalt ..." "Thou shalt not ..." All behavior is measured according to those tenets of faith.

Therein lies one of the major reasons for the experience of religious culture shock when MKs return to their home countries. Even shared core values will be lived out differently from one culture to another. For example, believers around the world may agree with the Biblical principle of dressing modestly,[3] but the way people define or express "modesty" can differ dramatically. One culture thinks nothing of seeing a woman wearing a halter top and very short shorts in a store. Another culture would throw that woman in jail for indecent exposure. It considers a woman immodest who shows any bare skin in public besides her eyes and hands.

How, then, do you figure out what is faith and what is culture? Or how does a group of people from one culture, living in another, decide on the culturally appropriate standards for practicing the principles of their faith?

Undoubtedly, this is one of those places where a third culture community definitely has its roots in the home culture. Missionaries arrive overseas with their own operative cultural expressions of faith. Take the example of modesty again. When missionaries came to Nigeria in the 1920s, few women in the States wore lipstick. Those who did were considered "wanton women." Flashy, dangly earrings served as another sign of this decadence. Because of that, American women who wished to be modest at that time wore neither lipstick nor earrings. This makeup-free custom took root in our subculture as a transplant of the norms prevailing in American culture at the time.

But not all of a religious third culture's customs come from the home country. Many are also shaped by the mores of the local community. In respect for what is considered modest in the surrounding cultures, missionary kids are often told what they can and can't wear. At the time I was growing up in Africa, Nigerian women openly breastfed their babies, but no woman bared her legs in public or would think of wearing something as form-fitting as slacks. None of these cultural rules applied in the States, but we female MKs wore only dresses during those early years in Nigeria. We didn't want to transgress local cultural norms.

From this mixture of messages, a new set of mores forms for the missionary subculture. Long after peers in the States wore lipstick with completely appropriate cultural modesty, most American women missionaries didn't because the "rule" had been established years before. As an adult, I lived in a missionary community in Liberia. By then, some Liberian women wore slacks for shopping and other events in town. Yet when a woman missionary wore slacks to a picnic, it touched off a furor among members in our mission community; this resulted in a new edict delineating exactly what was, and what was not, appropriate attire for all the community's members. The reasons for the rule about not wearing pants had long since been lost, but the rules were still operative. We had developed a culture unlike either the home or the host culture, but we all knew the rules for it. And this is what causes such a problem at reentry.

Although these written and unwritten rules originally emerge as attempts to express faith in a culturally appropriate way, as cultures change and rules remain unchanged the rules become synonymous with faith itself. In the end, they define who does or doesn't have faith. After I got past the lipstick and earrings on that pier in New York, my eyes bulged when I saw women shopping while wearing "short-shorts." Even more shocking were women at church socials in *pants!* How could they possibly do such things and claim to have the same faith as I did?

But in another way, that specific, rule-based culture shock is perhaps among the most minor ones MKs ultimately face. After seeing my confusion, Mom took time later to explain that wearing lipstick had nothing directly to do with faith. But since people had different opinions about it and the Bible also teaches us to live peacefully with others, we simply didn't wear it in Africa.

The far more difficult type of religious culture shock missionary kids experience relates to how substantive matters of doctrine—not just principles for behavior—are believed or expressed in the home churches compared to how the MK has always learned them. Differences in world views between cultures can result in markedly different interpretations of the same Scripture. For example, I grew up in a place where belief in spiritual powers, both good and evil, basically ruled everyday life. One form of power or the other could be invoked to take care of any situation needing some type of intervention. The Biblical accounts of demon-possession were no problem to believe because I commonly heard about demon-possessed people being set free by the power of God. It's just the way life was.

Upon returning to the States, I discovered that members of my own church explained away such Biblical accounts as "mental illness." They told me that this supposed demon possession actually represented an attempt by "superstitious people" to explain what we now recognize as mental illness. That presented a real problem for me. While I often wondered at the arrogance that presumed that only Americans and their "scientific" minds knew the true nature of this world, I also realized that the two opposing views couldn't both be right. How did I know which one to choose? These types of encounters ultimately shook me to the core of my faith. Again, this is a paradox, for while these problems made life confusing and difficult for some years, I finally had to determine whether I believed what I believe only because I'd been taught this way, or if, in fact, I believed because I truly *believe*. Whatever the final outcome of this process, it has lifelong consequences for MKs.

Another big difference between home and host cultures for many MKs is the intensity of how faith is expressed. I grew up seeing people's lives radically changed when they became Christians. In fact, many put their lives on the line to do so. To me, African Christians were brave, fearless believers who gloried in their newfound faith. In America, most Christians I knew then seemed to have been raised in the faith. They were glad about Jesus, but the radiant joy and excitement my African friends expressed about the overwhelming change in their lives often wasn't there.

A related shock for many MKs occurs when they come from countries where people openly talk about faith. In those places "Praise the Lord" or "If God is willing" are everyday expressions in normal conversation. Meanwhile, back "home" anything remotely relating to religion is considered intensely private.

Some religious culture shock, of course, is simply an extension of what TCKs in general face upon reentry. One MK, Grace, told me that her biggest problem in reentry was the ethnocentrism of her high school youth group at church. They seemed totally unaware of anything other than whatever issues affected their own group. She disliked the lack of racial or cultural diversity within the group. While this type of ethnocentrism is a common frustration for TCKs of all backgrounds, when it happens within a church community at home it takes on an added dimension for MKs. "If they really loved God like they're supposed to, they wouldn't behave like this."

Although Gwenda, another MK, admits to a frustration similar to what Grace felt when she encountered the ethnocentrism of her home church congregation, she dealt with it differently. "I became inwardly very arrogant," she said. "In my heart I'd say, 'Here they all are in fancy clothes and thinking they're so great, but they haven't a clue what's going on in the world.'" Instead of jumping into her church group, Gwenda stayed on the sidelines with a sense of superiority for what she knew and they didn't. While this type of arrogance is also typical of a general reentry experience, it becomes sanctified when missionary kids can justify it because they are also defending God's causes as they champion the cause of the poor and oppressed.

For David, an MK from India, the padded pews, plush carpets, and pipe organs of his church in the States seemed to put God at a far greater distance than worshipping under a thatched roof on a mud floor in his beloved India. Seeing males and females sitting together throughout the service amazed him. In India, males sat on the right side of the aisle, females on the left.

John, who grew up in Ghana, was bored by the services back in his home country. From his

African experience, he was used to drums and dancing in church throughout the long services. He loved the spontaneous clapping and antiphonal singing that went on until the story seemed told or the choir director decided it was enough. Now everything seemed so planned that there wasn't even room for a spontaneous "Amen" from the congregation. John's only problem was his father, who didn't seem to understand this change and continued saying "Amen" whenever he felt like it—much to John's embarrassment!

Of course, how churches and fellow believers spend money is a big issue for many MKs. They are used to working and living with the poor and being relatively poor themselves. To know that thousands of dollars are being spent to change the curtain colors or add a slightly bigger stove in the church's already seemingly well-equipped kitchen can seem unconscionable to an MK. "Why isn't that money being spent to feed the poor or pay for a blind man to get his cataract operation?" Some MKs stop going to church altogether over such things.

The difference in how religious holidays are expressed leaves many MKs feeling "blah" at Christmas and Easter. To come to a country where the religious significance of those two holidays is so completely secularized is a major culture shock. For me, Christmas had very precise steps in the celebration of Christ's birth. First, that's what it was— a celebration of His birth, not a season for Santa Claus. Second, it always began with inviting friends over for Christmas Eve and choosing exactly one gift to open under the Christmas tree, which was made from a plaster board cut in the shape of a pine tree, covered with green crepe paper, and hung on the wall with tinsel and a few ornaments. Third, we went to bed with great anticipation of the arrival of the angels (students from my dad's elementary school) who came to sing outside our home in the middle of the night to announce the Savior's birth. Certainly it wasn't hard to imagine what the shepherds had experienced on the Judean hillside long ago. Fourth, Christmas morning involved a drama at church, with my dad's striped housecoat serving as a costume for one of the shepherds. It all made the Christmas story alive and meaningful. And it wouldn't have been the same without the smell of the harmattan dust in the air.

David told me that at Christmas he missed sitting on the straw mats of his church in India the most. For him, that kind of atmosphere seemed far closer to the world where Christmas took place than a plush church in the United States.

For missionary TCKs, home leave is often another paradoxical experience. Because missionaries are generally supported through donations by friends and churches at home, missionary families spend much time visiting these often widely scattered friends and churches during their furloughs. The missionaries report on their work, thank those who have supported them, and look for new support.

Again, there are many benefits to this experience. I always felt incredibly special to our two main supporting churches—one in Minneapolis, one in Chicago. Those churches not only sent financial support to my parents, they became wonderfully involved with us as a family—sewing clothes for our next four years, sending packages filled with Cracker Jack and Double Bubble gum at Christmas, lavishing food and attention on us each time we came home. To this day, when I visit those churches, I am still "Ruth Ellen" to all the older members. I remain close friends with peers who took me into the high school youth group during the four years I lived with my grandma and aunt while my parents were in Nigeria. Certainly I feel great affection and warmth when I think of all the wonderful people in those churches.

The other side of the equation, however, is that those weren't the only churches that supported my parents. Perhaps there were thirty more—some giving $5.00 per month, some $10.00—but all had to be visited. Cross-country driving with six children in one car may be one way to see the world, but it gets very cramped. To hit a new home, new family, new church night after night or week after week during the months you weren't in school could get old pretty fast. It's one thing to sing "Yesu Yana Kamnar Yara" for one church; it's quite another thing to do so for thirty churches. After awhile it's no longer fun to be the new kid in the Sunday school class "who's from Africa," with the inevitable follow-up question, "Can you tell us what it was like?" When I lived in Nigeria, I never had to answer that question. Everyone I knew was also "from Africa."

While these types of questions are, of course, mildly annoying to most TCKs from all backgrounds, there is a reason these situations put a particular strain on MKs. This added factor relates to why MKs are in these situations in the first place—the matter of financial support. While parents from any sponsoring agency can lose a job if their TCKs misbehave in the host culture, when many third culture families return home for leave, how they live and what they choose to do with their time or financial resources either are nonissues or go unnoticed as they blend in with the greater anonymity of the home culture.

But because missionary families receive donations for their support, not only do MKs have to behave in the host cultures, but they have to keep a lot of people happy with them in order to go back at all. As the saying goes, "He who pays the piper calls the tune." And, because faith is expressed in so many cultural ways, when MKs don't know the local cultural mores it becomes easy to offend the donors who have been supporting their family. They've also learned that it doesn't always take much to offend. When my father died, a church that had supported my parents for over thirty years wrote Mom and told her they were dropping her support. Why? Because since Jesus told His disciples to go out two-by-two, they couldn't support someone who would now be going out one-by-one! Other friends of mine attempted frugality by giving up their car for a tandem bike. They figured out how to arrange their family of five on the seats and handlebars to get around the mile-square mission station. When they wrote of this happy solution to their transportation needs, a donor family dropped their monthly $100 support. The reason? The supporting family said they were scrimping to send this money each month and couldn't possibly afford a bicycle-built-for-two. If the missionaries had so much extra money that they could afford such a luxury, they obviously no longer needed the family's support. When an MK grows up with such stories, no one has to tell him or her how essential good behavior is during furloughs.

Sometimes this role as a little ambassador for Jesus, or at least for their family finances, continues even when MKs return to the overseas post. Denise Vibbert Patch catches the dilemma and frustration masterfully in her article, "Hope You Get Your CYC Badge." She begins by telling of her frustration that people never know anything about Burundi when she mentions that she lived there for five years. Then she goes on to say:

Most of the time the conversation doesn't get much farther than that. These people are still curious, but they're too inhibited to voice their true questions. What they don't know is that I know what they're thinking They are the adults who used to write to me when we were all children.

> Dear Denise,
>
> Hi. How are you doing? I am O.K. Do you eat food? Do you wear clothes? Please write back.
>
> Love, Timmy.

At first it was fun to get mail from American kids. Letters addressed to me. For a fourth grader that's a pretty big deal. But after about six months and thirty-some letters, it wasn't fun anymore.

One afternoon I was sitting at the dining room table with a stack of airforms and a pencil. I had completed my home schooling assignments before lunch, and now it was two o'clock and I wanted to go for a bike ride.

"Just write a few sentences on the back of the form letter and then you can go. And Denise," my mom paused with a warning look.

"Yeh?" I tried to look innocent.

"Be nice." Though I had never carried out my threat to write my true reactions to these letters,

I think my mom could sense I was really getting insulted by these kids.

I didn't answer. Instead I bent my head and scrawled:

Dear Ann,

Thank you for writing to me. It's a lot of fun for me to sit and answer your dumb questions. I could be out riding my bike and chasing lions. I hope you get your CYC badge. Then you won't have to write to me again. That would be nice. Tell all your CYC friends some things for me. First, I don't live in a house. My dad builds a fire every night and we sleep around it on mats. Second, I do not eat food. Not many missionaries do. God makes it so we're never hungry. Third, I don't wear clothes. I like it better being naked. Fourth, we do not have Christmas. I think Jesus was only born for Americans. Fifth, I don't have any friends. That's why I get so happy when you write to me. Sixth, I do not speak English. If you have any more question about my weirdness please write them in Hunga Bunga. I'm sure you'll still get your badges for trying.

Love, Denise.[4]

At the end of the article, of course, Denise doesn't send this letter and instead writes, "Dear Ann, Thank you for writing me. It's really not that different living in Burundi ..." Still, this episode does express the frustration some MKs feel with the sense that they must always report to the church folks back home and keep them happy.

Writing about my root system for this article has been both edifying and difficult. Edifying as I remember the great strengths I received from such a strong community. Difficult as I wonder if my readers will understand that or only see the apparent foibles. A friend of mine recently questioned her son's teacher about using a particular book on Native American Indians for his fourth grade reading class. The book contained an extensive discussion of religious rituals as well as a discourse on religious beliefs. My friend wondered how that book could be used when similar books on other religions could not.

The teacher replied, "Well, it is impossible to have any discussion of the Native American Indians without a discussion of religion because that is a central part of their whole culture."

That's how it is for the missionary community. Times have certainly changed since my days as an MK. Many missionaries live scattered in rented houses throughout the cities and towns where they work rather than on mission compounds. Short-termers abound, so many MKs no longer spend a lifetime in one place as I did. Schooling patterns have changed. Missions themselves have become internationalized.

But one thing hasn't changed—the reason they went. Missionaries believe God has asked them to do this. That underlying reason still guides and shapes everything else. Perhaps, in the end, understanding and respecting that core foundation still causes me the greatest dissonance when I am back in my own culture. For many Americans, the idea that a person would sacrifice personal pleasure and comfort for such a reason seems almost mockable.

"Probably it's just a bad case of co-dependency," or "They couldn't make it here anyway." And I think, "You really don't know, do you?" Yes, there are failings and shortcomings as in any community, but perhaps the greatest gift I've received as an MK is that of watching people who have dared to live for something grander, something more than their own comfort and pleasure. It's not always so easy to find here at home anymore. I'm glad I've seen it somewhere.

Notes

1. Ruth Hill Useem, "Third Cultural Factors in Educational Change," in *Cultural Factors in School Learning*, ed. Cole Brembeck and Walker Hiler (Lexington, MA: D. C. Heath, 1973), p. 122.

2. Mary Ellen Wertsch, *Military Brats: Legacies of Childhood Inside the Fortress* (Bayside, NY: Aletheia Publications, 1996).

3. I Timothy 2:9-10.

4. Denise Vibbert Patch, "I Hope You Get Your CYC Badge," *Quest* (Spring Arbor College, Spring Arbor, MI), October 1989.

Understanding Global Nomads

Norma M. McCaig

NORMA M. MCCAIG, *a cross-cultural consultant, trainer, and writer, is the founder of Global Nomads International, a not-for-profit membership organization in association with the United Nations that provides services and publications for global nomads of any age or nationality, assists their families and sponsoring organizations, and increases awareness of the global nomad in the larger community. The daughter of an international business executive, she grew up in the Philippines, Sri Lanka, and India.*

I CAN STILL HEAR the wind from the dust storm that hit Delhi that May: resonant vowels of nature's voice rising and falling, finding closure in a consonant hum like the chant of an ancient mantra. Powerful images from Coaker's Walk, farther south in India, nearer my childhood school in Kodaikanal, Tamil Nadu, become equally vivid: seventy-odd picnicking street children and orphans striking exaggerated, unsteady classical dance poses and collapsing in mirth around me, on me, with shining eyes and soft little hands. Memories of that chance two-hour encounter on the edge of a mountain and in another world are a source of both pain and wonder: pain at having said yet another goodbye in the cool Palni Hills sanctuary above the sun-seared plains; wonder at the circumstances that brought me to that moment.

I am acutely aware that had I not been given a childhood overseas, these and other remembrances from both the distant and the recent past would likely not exist. They are indelibly part of my heritage and my legacy as a global nomad, someone who has lived abroad as a child as a consequence of a parent's job.

The benefits of this upbringing need to be underscored: In an era when global vision is an imperative, when skills in intercultural communication, linguistic ability, mediation, diplomacy, and the management of diversity are critical, global nomads are better equipped in these areas by the age of eighteen than are many adults. Why? Because they have spent years developing these skills as strategies for social survival in times of transition. Without them they would be unable to gain social entry into international or host culture children's groups when moving from one overseas post to another.

These intercultural and linguistic skills are the markings of the cultural chameleon—the young participant-observer who takes note of verbal and nonverbal cues and readjusts accordingly, taking on enough of the coloration of the social surroundings to gain acceptance while maintaining some vestige of identity as a different animal, an "other." With plenty of time for practice provided during their impressionable childhood years, global nomads often become keen observers of human behavior, developing the invaluable ability to suspend judgment while examining both sides of an issue or situation. In addition, they learn the skill of social extraversion necessary to becoming part of a group quickly and often appreciate diversity to the point of consciously seeking it later in life. Mind you, all this is largely done unconsciously. Yet these very skills, a natural part of the global nomad's heritage, are critically needed in today's world of ethnically diverse national populations and fluid cultural and political borders.

The ease with which young global nomads cruise global corridors often gives rise to an expanded world view, the capacity to extend their vision beyond national boundaries. This ability "to view the world whole," as noted interculturalist Margaret Pusch has said, is one of the salient and most valuable assets global nomads have to offer to the communities they inhabit from young adulthood on, and sometimes before. Given their uniquely acquired knowledge, intercultural and linguistic communication skills, and attitudes born of a globally peripatetic childhood, global nomads come to maturity well equipped with a foundation for effecting change—locally and nationally and, certainly, globally.

That global nomads use their skills beyond childhood is confirmed by recent research on adult TCKs by a team that includes Dr. Ruth Hill Useem, who pioneered research focusing on TCKs in the early 1960s. This study-in-progress reveals that

> most (over 75 percent) actively participate
> in their local community or in a broader

network ... (PTA, sports, scouts, etc.) and their church. About half (47 percent) of those who report volunteer activities include an international dimension, such as participating in organizations such as the United Nations Association; hosting exchange students; or translating in courts, schools, or hospitals.[1]

The researchers also note that global nomads

relate [U.S.] Americans to the rest of the world and interpret the outside world to the immediate world in which they live. Significant proportions of them actually do this for a living.[2]

They are, as Dr. Ted Ward maintains, "the prototype citizens of the twenty-first century." Not bad fallout from a parent's job.

This sense of having been given the world as a learning ground through an accident of birth and the intrepid, adventuresome spirit of one's parent or parents is shared by hundreds of grown and nearly-grown global nomads with whom I have spoken during the past ten years. Few would opt to have been born and reared in Hometown, U.S.A.

And yet, the gift of a global childhood is sometimes costly. It is not uncommon for global nomads to express some sense of rootlessness, to feel perpetually out of step or marginalized, to be somewhat indecisive and noncommittal, and to either resist deeper levels of intimacy or have difficulty establishing and maintaining long-term relationships. Occasionally these feelings are played out in the form of alcohol and/or drug abuse, eating disorders, depression, and other dysfunctional behavior. These may appear during the overseas posting, but are more likely to manifest themselves as TCKs make the transition from life abroad to life at "home." Many parents are surprised at the metamorphosis of their wonderfully compliant, pleasant teenager into a rebellious, petulant, angry, withdrawn or irresponsible adolescent upon returning "home." This change is even more astonishing when it occurs in the twentysomething-year-old who is supposed to be "beyond all that."

What follows is an exploration of the characteristics and dynamics of the globally nomadic family and the spheres of cultural impact on the global nomad to provide a basis for understanding the reasons. Included as well are some effective strategies for parent-child interaction in the special context of the internationally mobile lifestyle.

Characteristics and Dynamics of the Family Abroad

NOT surprisingly, the sponsored family abroad (diplomatic, military, missionary, etc.) is better educated than the average geographically stable family. Of comfort to parents are research findings by Useem and her colleagues revealing that 81 percent of grown nomads (versus 21 percent in the U.S. population) earned, at minimum, a bachelor's degree, with a full half of them completing master's and doctoral programs.[3]

Another characteristic of parents of global nomads is that theirs is a chosen lifestyle: At least one partner is highly motivated to make the best of it, and generally both are. In this way the global nomad's family differs from immigrant and refugee families, whose internationally mobile lifestyle may be thrust upon them by sudden or chronic external circumstances such as poverty or political upheaval. It is important to understand, however, that within the global nomad's family this sense of choice may not—in fact often is not—shared by the children. During childhood global nomads often respond with what appears to be great resiliency. However, many adult global nomads report a sense of powerlessness and devaluation when reflecting on their upbringing.

Many parents living abroad share the sense that they are always navigating new waters, in that they must manage child-rearing while moving in and out of a variety of geographic, professional, social, and cultural environments. Many feel somewhat prepared for duty in a specific place, but some feel less prepared for what is to be an internationally mobile family *over time*—ten or twenty years, through numerous moves over two or more continents and the birth of several children, each perhaps in a different corner of the globe.

Parents from a monocultural background with little or no experience of mobility are often doubly handicapped. Many feel thrust into a global existence without a roadmap for parenting. Adding to their distress is the fact that many grandparents actively disapprove of the frequent moves of their grandchildren, who, in their minds, are likely to be spoiled by an unrealistically privileged lifestyle while being exposed to constant danger of attack by everything from microbes to terrorists. Such lack of family support can intensify the expatriate parent's sense of isolation while abroad.

For globally nomadic families, the extended family and longtime friends become essentially inaccessible. These people, who are such an integral part of the parents' lives, may become almost as one-dimensional as pictures in someone else's family album. More important, it means that a significant safety valve for siphoning off family tensions is shut down because children can no longer be sent to stay with grandparents while their parents resolve a problem or crisis. Nor can they go down the block to blow off steam or seek advice from a trusted childhood friend. Other support systems need to be developed to supplant reliance on relatives and lifelong friends.

The upside of this is the opportunity to develop one's own style of handling situations and to create networks while drawing on existing resources in the expatriate community, such as workshops, counseling, books, and other materials provided by the sponsoring organization.

Yet another significant characteristic of the globally nomadic family is the high degree of interdependence among family members—heavy reliance on one another as the most important source of emotional support and validation. Given their mobile lifestyle, family members are psychologically thrown back on one another in a way that is not typical in geographically stable families. The nuclear family is the only social unit that is constant through time in the lives of an internationally mobile family.

Close family bonds are not uncommon. Siblings may become each other's best friend. Parents may as well. Patterns formed overseas may fly in the face of conventional theory about when children leave home, both emotionally and physically. Research may one day prove that they do so on another timetable from that of the geographically rooted family member. The developmental task of separation may end up being postponed for two reasons: (1) handling transitions from post to post requires reliance on the support of the nuclear family, and (2) the teenager may not be willing to trade the only known, consistent source of support—the family—for a place in a community of international transients, a community he or she will probably leave shortly as well. Hence the "delayed adolescent rebellion" of the twentysomething-year-old referred to earlier, which may also be due in part to unresolved grief.

Clearly, the strength of this family bond works to the benefit of children when the parents' marriage is sound, communication is good, and overall family dynamics are healthy. Compared to the geographically stable child, the globally nomadic child is inordinately reliant on the nuclear family for affirmation, behavior modeling, support, and above all, safety. The impact, therefore, of dysfunction in this most basic of units is exacerbated by a highly mobile existence. Constant unresolved family tension can become chronically debilitating. Physical, sexual, and emotional abuse, sometimes prompted by alcohol abuse or depression, may go unnoticed or unacknowledged by friends, acquaintances, and educators for a variety of reasons: misguided notions about "respecting privacy," lack of opportunity for long-term observation, fear of repatriation, or family disgrace.

Children themselves may be reticent about revealing abuse or chronic tension, for any of a number of reasons: (1) It is so chronic that it feels normal; (2) in the child's mind, at least one parent must know what is happening and condone it, and therefore the child must deserve it; or (3) the child consciously or unconsciously denies feelings of abandonment and abuse in an effort to shore up the myth of a happy childhood. The Brady Bunch illusion must be kept intact for the sake of emotional survival.

Although such coping strategies are used by many children, rooted or not, the point is that dysfunction can cut deeper into the heart of the global nomad child because of the family's transient lifestyle and relative emotional isolation.

Finally, when parents from a relatively monocultural, geographically stable background step on the plane with their children for a life abroad they become a bicultural family, one that may well be on its way to becoming a multicultural family. Why? Because the context of the parents' upbringing and that of their children will vary vastly. A first child may teethe in Uganda, tie a first shoelace in

Belgium, and come of age in Thailand. In the process, of course, these children are absorbing and internalizing observations about human interaction in a variety of cultural contexts.

In addition, the countries in which subsequent children are born, tie shoelaces, and come of age may vary from one child to the next, thus shaping the children in a family somewhat differently from each other. In the end, each child's story of life abroad—the sharpest memories, cultural images, and most significant events—may read like pages from a separate book.

Dual-culture children, whose parents are of different nationalities or ethnicities, obviously are in a bicultural family during this extended adventure abroad. The cultural dynamic between such spouses and among family members, then, may provide yet another overlay to be taken into account as the child's cultural identity and concept of "home" are being constructed.

Spheres of Cultural Influence

CLEARLY there are many cultural forces that can take the global nomad in a number of fascinating and enriching directions. They include the culture of educational systems in different posts, the caregiver's culture, various host cultures, the parents' culture(s) of origin, the majority expatriate community culture, and the culture of the sponsoring community (diplomatic, military, business, missionary, etc.), to name a few.

The educational sphere of influence demands close attention. Curricula designed to meet the needs of a specific national school system reflect not only the academic standards of that country but also its cultural norms, the language in which classes are taught, and its style of learning and patterns of thinking. Thus children who move from one educational system to another need time to adjust to differences and may require tutoring and extra classes in order to qualify for their next academic step.

World Bank educational consultant Ethna Hopper tells the story of a father who complained that his son lacked motivation and seemed sullen. No wonder, she noted. He was "in his fourth country, fourth school system, learning in his fourth language." In short, the boy was tired.

The easiest option, of course, is to choose one educational system and maintain it from post to post. This may be of particular importance for parents of a child who generally finds adapting to new situations and contexts difficult, or of a learning-disabled child for whom resources at most schools are sorely limited. The more adventuresome child who is innately more flexible may respond well to, and indeed benefit from, experiencing more than one system in the course of a childhood abroad.

The degree to which a child is affected by the host culture depends on a number of variables: length of stay, degree of contact with host nationals, the size of both the sponsoring and expatriate communities, and the willingness of parents to encourage children to engage the culture and its people. Perhaps the strongest connection, both culturally and emotionally, that a child can have to a host country is through a caregiver. Often this person imparts language, cultural behavior, and, to some degree, values to the child, depending on the child's age.

Considering the variety of cultural influences on a child at just *one* post and multiplying them by the three or more posts many children move to during their time abroad conveys the magnitude of the factors that shape the heart, soul, mind, and identity of the global nomad, both as a child and as an adult. Small wonder, then, that the global nomad child often finds transition to his or her passport country to be a startling experience at best.

The Transition "Home"

THE process of returning to the passport country deserves special attention. While parents are re-entering, children step off the plane "riding on their parents' mythology of home," as global nomad Timothy Dean notes. As one mother put it, "For my children, home is just another somewhere."

It is at this point that differences in cultures and expectations between parent and child become most apparent. As noted transition and family consultant David Pollock often says, parents returning to their country of origin are coming home; their children are leaving home. There is no doubt that parents are changed by their international sojourning and certainly experience the impact of reentry; nevertheless, they are usually on more familiar cultural and geographic ground, owing to their rooted upbringing in that culture, than are their offspring. Their children's culture, on the other hand, is basically an international one with an overlay of the passport culture. They therefore often feel like hidden immigrants when they reach "home." Because they look and talk as if they should belong, their outlook, actions, and lack of knowledge of local and cultural trivia are often bewildering to those around them who do not know (or care) that they have lived abroad. At the other extreme, the child may be put on a pedestal by young friends—highly valued as unique, but not necessarily made "one of the gang." In either situation, the results are similar: The child is left on the outside looking in, skirting the margins of the group along with the druggies and geeks.

In terms of timing, research tells us that transitions occurring during the early adolescent years (ages twelve to fourteen) can be particularly tough on children. Their task can be made easier by parents and extended family members who (1) are willing to accept the fact that they are *of another culture* by virtue of their childhood abroad, (2) are realistic about how and when they will assimilate, and (3) encourage *them* to be realistic. Here is what the research team of Drs. Useem and Useem, Cottrell, and Jordan discovered:

> The answer to the question of how long it takes them to adjust to American life is: They never adjust. They adapt, they find niches,

they take risks, they fail and pick themselves
up again.... As one woman put it, "I don't
feel different, I AM different."[4]

For global nomads, this is not a phase but a
state of being. Putting the high expectation of total adjustment on them (complete with a set time
frame for doing so) is as unreasonable as asking
a Kenyan who might have spent time in college in
the United States to "become a typical U.S. American." Global nomads who feel forced to disown
their valuable heritage in the name of "fitting in"
lose, as do their communities.

Provided with an environment that not only
acknowledges but also values their experience and
encourages them to use their skills, global nomads
can—and many will—change the world they live in.

Parenting Strategies

ISSUES related to cultural identity and high mobility are dominant themes in the life of the globally nomadic family. How can parents most
effectively guide children under these circumstances? Some useful strategies follow.

COMMUNICATION

KEEPING the lines of communication open is as
challenging as it is obvious; not only between par-

ent and child, but also between spouses. Children are like lightning rods for parental discord and family tension. This is especially true of children abroad, who miss almost nothing. A study of German diplomatic families by Dr. Stephan Hormuth directly correlates the success of the child's adaptation to a new post to the success of the mother's adaptation.

It is important to encourage children to talk about their lives, about their reactions, feelings, observations. It is equally important to accept or challenge what they say in the spirit of developing their skills in critical thinking rather than as a means of judging or controlling them. Keep reminding yourself about the difference between discipline (guidance) and punishment (power) and the effects of each on parent-child communication.

COLLABORATION

MANY global nomad children feel that they have little control over their lives. Withholding from children the knowledge of an impending transfer until shortly before the packers come does not spare them pain, it magnifies it. There is no time to adjust to the thought of moving; what should be a normal international move feels more like an evacuation.

Transfers can, in fact, make the global nomad child feel like a piece of luggage carried on and off planes at fairly regular intervals: Whatever

feelings of attachment have been formed seem to
be devalued and considered expendable. For some
global nomads eating disorders, particularly
anorexia, can be a manifestation of a need to control *something* in their lives when the stress and
ambiguities of an international lifestyle crowd in.
Unwillingness or inability to commit or set goals
in later adolescence and beyond may be related
to early feelings of powerlessness. One way to deal
with that is to include the child as much as possible—and as early as possible—in the family decision-making process.

CONTINUITY

WHEN packing to leave a place, allow your child
to choose which "sacred objects" to take and
which items to give away. Like furniture, photo-
graphs, and family rituals, "sacred objects" are a
form of continuity. They are the outward and vis-
ible signs of a family's heritage. They become the
glue holding the pieces of former lives together
with those found in new places. In our family, we
could always count on having waffles on Sunday
night, wherever we were. Three decades later, each
time I use a little syrup pitcher I am taken back to
a different "there."

If you are a single parent, or a dual-career
couple, tenaciously guard your time with your
children. Relying too heavily on an ayah or nanny
in an overseas setting can heighten a child's sense
of abandonment.

In a highly mobile lifestyle, friendships sometimes seem short-lived, yet many adult global nomads report that the renewal of old friendships is a source of unexpected joy and continuity. To help maintain friendships over time and space, on birthdays and other special occasions some parents give their children the gift of a free telephone call to any friend anywhere in the world. It's expensive, but it works! Such efforts encourage global nomads to view their sense of rootedness using other than conventional constructs: They are not rootless, they are rooted in a different way—through people rather than places.

That global nomads share a common heritage with other global nomads is clear when they meet. Regardless of their passport country, the countries lived in, the parents' sponsoring agency, age, or any number of other variables, there is a sudden recognition of kinship, a sense of homecoming that underlines the powerful bond created by their shared culture. Each has more in common with the other than with those who have not had a childhood abroad.

More and more opportunities for maintaining continuity with the global nomads in a number of U.S. cities are becoming available. Global Nomads Puget Sound in Washington State and Global Nomads Washington Area on the East Coast are two examples of U.S. groups offering opportunities for socializing, career networking, focused discussion, and outreach. Similar groups have been formed in Finland, Norway, Holland, and Japan. Universities and colleges, including George Mason University, Duke University, the

University of Virginia, and at least ten others, recognize the value of encouraging the formation of
global nomad clubs on campus. GMU and Duke
now include U.S. global nomads in their definition of *international student* and are in the forefront
of providing academic, career, and psychological
services for global nomads with counselors who
are knowledgeable about the dynamics of a childhood abroad.

Organizations like Mu Kappa, primarily for
missionary kids, and Global Nomads International,
for global nomads of any age or nationality, provide a means for joining a wider international network. Through efforts and organizations like these,
global nomads can be assisted in effecting a
healthy integration of their unique past into both
their present and their future.

CLOSURE

WITH as many uprootings and replantings as internationally mobile families experience, many
parents are either unaware of the need for closure or unwilling or afraid to address it before
moving on. Most of us have developed some effective strategies for coping with the discomfort
of separation. As a child, mine was "See you in
the States!"

Many global nomads go through more grief
experiences before the age of eighteen than others do in a lifetime. Pollock captures the powerful
impact of these experiences in five key words: He

notes that the global nomad's grief is *multiple* (it happens over and over again); *simultaneous* (saying goodbye to friends, teachers, household staff, places, smells, sounds, foods, languages, etc., at the same time); *intense* (because many of these are loved or valued); *unresolved* (unless the grieving process has been acknowledged and permitted to run its course); and *lonely* (regardless of where the child next steps off the plane, there are likely few people, other than the parents, whom the child trusts enough to share this sadness with).

When one's sense of loss is left unacknowledged and unattended, a natural emotional process is thwarted. Done enough times, Pollock says, it can kick back in the form of diffused depression, anger, or another dysfunctional expression.

Sometimes parents who are struggling with their own feelings of grief find it difficult to address those same feelings in their children. Sometimes being confronted with their children's anger and pain is difficult, particularly given the fact that the pain is generated by the parents' choice of lifestyle. Sometimes parents feel that this lifestyle is a valuable gift to their children (which it certainly can be), that leaving is a part of life, and that they should be looking forward to the next chapter rather than trying to close the book.

Giving children permission to express their sadness at leaving treasured friends and places is key. Many books on the grief process talk of stages, such as denial, anger, and acceptance, all of which may occur when global nomads move to new posts or back to the States.

CULTURAL CONFIRMATION

THE issue of cultural identity is perhaps the greatest potential source of conflict between parents and global nomad children. U.S. Foreign Service life in particular underlines the necessity for diplomats to maintain their "U.S. Americanness" to properly represent the country while abroad. Conversely, their children (while well aware of their role as miniature ambassadors) are absorbing this wider environment in another way, one that emphasizes cultural flexibility and reinforces a global perspective. Some may be drawn to host cultures that more nearly fit their personalities and values than does American culture. Others may choose to be citizens of the world, continuing to be globally peripatetic as adults.

On a cultural continuum with total identification with the United States at one extreme and total identification as a world citizen at the other, each child in a globally nomadic family may choose to alight at a different point. One child may choose a dual-culture marriage. Another may be unhappy in U.S. society and may leave at the first opportunity. Whereas this may be conventionally viewed as "failure to adjust," is it really so? All parents are called upon to let their children go; for the globally nomadic parent this may mean letting them go to another continent and way of life as well. This means understanding that children may not be "going native"; they may be going home. Those who choose to stay in the United States may express ideas and hold values that many may regard as unpatriotic. Some may give an impression of being "permanently temporarily here," but not fully "at home."

Guiding global nomads as they come to their decisions is, of course, critical. It is essential to recognize that their sense of cultural identity may be compartmentalized, global, or specific to another country.

Brian Lev has eloquently summed up the impact of life as a global nomad:

> Even now that I'm "thirtysomething," I find myself reacting to the world as a nomad. I hate to find my mailbox empty, even though my friends are (usually) only a phone call away; I have no room in my basement because I can't make myself throw away all those perfectly good empty packing boxes; the walls in my house are bare because I just *know* I'll just have to pack again soon; I still get a really bad case of wanderlust every four years or so (coinciding with the average Foreign Service tour of duty); and the dirtiest word I know is "goodbye."

About his perspective, Lev says,

> Even my best friends often shake their heads and change the subject when I find their point of views too ethno- or Americentric; I sometimes [think] everyone around me [views] the world in a terribly simplistic... way; and (while I have adopted certain aspects of it as my own) I find much of the U.S. culture limited in its scope. In addition,

I still have no way to describe these feelings
to even the closest of my friends.

On the concept of home, Lev is particularly
forceful:

After having to depend on myself so many
times in the past, my "home" is made up of
those memories and emotions I have collected over time from which I can draw comfort and strength as needed. In effect,
"home" is the place I can go in my mind
where culture is a mix from many places
and belonging can be taken for granted....
It's as if we [global nomads] have replaced
the physical "home" [of] non-nomads...with
an internal "home" we can go to when we
need a respite from the world.

Finally, he asks, "Are we really on the outside looking in, like a wanderer gazing longingly
through the window of a warm house on a cold
night? I perfer to think of us as looking out at the
world from a place inside ourselves that we share
with other nomads."

Notes

1.   *NewsLinks* (International Schools Services newsletter),
March 1994.
2.   *NewsLinks*, May 1993.
3.   Ibid.
4.   Ibid.

Rail Ways
Amy Rukea Stempel

AMY RUKEA STEMPEL is an American global nomad who grew up in Africa, Asia, and the Middle
East. A recipient of a 1993 Library of Congress Pro-
mising Young Poet Award, she is a poet, teacher, and
student of the humanities.

Station

Standing primed to view
the horizons of my soul
on a decaying, yellowing platform
bathed in equatorial dust
made gold by the plummeting sun

myself an exhibition
white in a land of brown
blond in a land of black
unable to completely blend
to gracefully bend with the
millennial noise of the living

vendors drift languidly in and out
a contrast to their insistent calls of commerce
sari draped women and lungi clad men
wrestle sleeping children
and mammoth cloth bags
to their claimed spot on the cracked cement

Train

The lowing of the whistle
reminds me of the sound my heart made
the moment it was broken
and lulls me to its side
the familiar ache of a soul well worn
with passion and peace

I reach for the familiar touch
of the railing worn by millions of offering
     hands
clasping and pulling to me
the love hate relationship
of challenger and challenged
seer and seen

A berth waits for me
the throne of my desire
to see the world through a different lens
as though it were my courtesan
as bedraggled and lame
as the beggar who stands at the window

Moving first slowly
like water coming to a boil
then seething along the tracks
the TV screen of my window
moves from people to trees to bare brown earth
this iron box contains the jewels of my worth

Tracks

Thousands upon thousands
of kilometers of track
stitches sewn by the drunk hand of a depressed
    doctor
unsure of his patient's survival
stitches healing wounds
aroused by distance

And difference
curing nothing
but remaining like the last kiss of a lost love
as a promise, a hope
that what was done can be undone
that words spoken need not remain indelibly
    seared upon the brain

concealed in the bowels of this giant worm
we could be fleeing from
we could be riding with
we could be colliding into
our souls as they were
the moment of our birth

Journey

Days pass shooting across countryside
long forgotten, easily remembered, never before
    seen
as though imprinted on my divinity
the moment I dropped
through the celestial portal
into the hands of my waiting humanity

transporting memories
like one thousand tons of gravel
to be dumped at the feet of everyone I have
    ever known
to sift through the fingers
of those waiting at a station
to receive me

my spirit splinters with every mile
unable to hold its joy
unwilling to hold its pain
metal bands and wooden ties wrap my chest
held in place by the thin, black, silk chord
of the distant suspiration
of a train approaching my station

Amy Rukea Stempel
April 1993

Growing Up
in the Military*

Morten G. Ender

MORTEN G. ENDER is an assistant professor of sociology and peace studies at the University of North Dakota. He is also principal investigator for the Adult Children of Military and Other Families Project, a research study carried out by the Department of Sociology at the university. Born in Germany into an Army family, he arrived in the United States aboard a troop ship and subsequently lived in Colorado, Kansas, Arizona, and California as well as in Nuremberg and Munich. His recent research has focused on the uses of traditional and new communications media by military families during war separations.

---

*An earlier version of this chapter was presented at the Eastern Sociological Society Meetings, Philadelphia, Pennsylvania, March 1995. The research was supported in part by a Faculty Research Grant through the Office of Research and Program Development, University of North Dakota, Grand Forks, North Dakota, under Contract No. 1813-2208-2017. The author wishes to thank Melissa Anderson, Ralph Kuhn, and Joan Natoli for their research assistance and Brenda Kowalewski, Corina Morano-Ender, and Carolyn Smith for their helpful and insightful comments on earlier drafts of this chapter.

IN HER STUDY OF a military community in Ankara, Turkey, Charlotte Wolf notes:

> As these Americans have been transported,
> so have their institutions, their culture, and
> many of their material accouterments. With
> such social and economic self-sufficiency,
> ethnic communal enclaves have developed
> within the foreign milieus. And the every-
> day routine of American children going to
> American schools, American fathers going
> to American jobs, American mothers shop-
> ping at American stores goes on in places
> as distant as Tokyo and Heidelberg, Izmir
> and Naha, Reykjavik and Manila. Like small
> alien islands in seas of foreign culture, these
> communities tenaciously maintain their dis-
> tinctive way of life.

She was describing a major and widespread phenomenon.

Beginning with World War II, American political, military, corporate, and humanitarian responsibilities greatly expanded outside U.S.
borders, and many Americans moved and lived
overseas. Government officials, soldiers, business
executives, and missionaries moved with their
families overseas in ever-increasing numbers.

By the end of the 1980s, the U.S. armed
forces had transitioned to a new politico-military
posture in light of the end of the Cold War. With
this shift, the U.S. and other Western militaries
have restructured and reduced their forces. However, the Cold War legacy has left a distinctive

imprint on the people who came of age within those military and other organization families.

In 1990, 5.5 million men and women were on active duty, retired from, or in a reserve component of the U.S. armed forces. The 2 million active duty military personnel had some 1,625,111 children not yet twenty-one years of age. One-fourth of these soldiers lived outside the United States. One consequence of the Cold War is this large pool of adult children from U.S. military and similar families. A conservative estimate would be 2 million. This essay will compare and contrast some of the advantages and disadvantages of this group and present some results of an ongoing study of this unique population of Americans.

Military Brats: The Persistent Negative Label

MILITARY *brat* is a label used to identify children, adolescents, youth, and adults from military families. No one is quite sure where the term originated, but it has persisted across this century. We do know that this somewhat derogatory label has been perpetuated in popular films such as *The Great Santini* and in a number of recent books such as: *Military Brats: Legacies of Childhood Inside the Fortress; Army Brat: A Memoir;* and *Brats: Children of the Military Speak Out.* Even those in the helping professions have used the label to title their books—*Psychiatry and the Army Brat.* The label has also appeared in the names of associations such as Overseas Brats, Military Brats of

America, Inc., Military Brats, Inc., and Canadian
Military Brats.

Most of the professional research on growing up in military families has contributed to the
perpetuation of the "brat" label. First, most of the
early studies of military families were reacting to
evidence of psychological pathology. Second, research from a psychiatric and psychological rather
than a sociological perspective has a long tradition of being generously supported by the military. Third, social problems within military families
have been attributed to the pathologies of individual family members or the family itself rather
than to characteristics of the military organization. Finally, a review of the scholarly studies published by researchers during the 1950s through
the early 1980s clearly shows the negative effects
of the military lifestyle outweighing the positive
effects. It is no wonder that the label endures and
is as popular as ever.

The Military Lifestyle: Demands of Work and Family

MORE recently, social science researchers in the
United States and abroad, especially sociologists,
are challenging some of the ideas that led to individuals being termed "brats" without recognizing
the effects of the military lifestyle on children. One
way to examine growing up in a military family is
to study the demands imposed by the military at
the intersection of work and family. These demands include (1) separation of one of the parents from the home for extended periods of time;

(2) complete and frequent family relocations; (3) living overseas for a number of years; and (4) an eventual transition to civilian life, among others. In addition, we know that many adults raised in military families came of age during the Vietnam War, and while their parents may have been pro-soldier, many of their peers were not. Collectively, these social elements are unique to the military experience. In addition, by focusing on the work/family intersection, the specific problems of individuals might be better understood. This approach takes the focus off of individuals and refocuses on the work and family situation. This approach also provides lessons for adults raised in other organizational family contexts such as international businesses, professors teaching abroad, missionaries, and the foreign service.

SEPARATION

THE often-recurring cycle of parental departure, interim absence, and reunion, as required for training, war, and other military operations, is a social reality for military families. Researchers have found separation to be a major developmental disruption for children, especially for boys. The adverse effects of a military father being absent could include low scholastic aptitude, health symptoms, behavior problems, and difficulties with sex-role identification. Because a number of influences can be related to how children respond to an absent father, the data are inconsistent. For example, some positive effects on child development also may occur in terms of opportunities for individual responsibility and a pleasurable home life with fewer parental restrictions.

For adolescents, separation from parents may not be as traumatic as for younger children. The adolescent, seeking more individual assertiveness at this stage of development, may take the absence of a parent as an opportunity to acquire more individual responsibility in and around the household. A father's absence may be especially positive for female adolescents, as the masculine culture of military service appears to frustrate the maturing feminine identity.

GEOGRAPHIC MOBILITY

GEOGRAPHIC mobility is ever present in American society. During the Cold War, military personnel relocated approximately every three years during their careers. Currently, there is conflicting evidence regarding the effects of relocation on children. Most of the early research was psychopathological in nature, using case studies to generalize to the population under study. Those studies emphasized negative effects of relocation, which include low self-esteem and behavioral difficulties. Some researchers have found that moving has positive effects on childhood development. Others suggest that the positive experience is not correlated with the move itself, but with the level of socialization the parents provide their children in preparing them for and supporting them before, during, and after the move. Other researchers have found both positive and negative effects related to parental attitude and guidance during moves. In this case, problems found in children may be a result of parents' inability to cope with their own stresses of moving. In other words, as go the parents, so go the children.

Moving is the most stressful experience for adolescents from a military community. The adolescent period of development is characterized by dissociating oneself from childhood yearnings and increasing cognitive development through exploration of social, interpersonal, and intimate relationships with peers. The family move represents a discontinuity in social relationships during the period when the individual's identity is emerging. One might assume that because civilians experience fewer moves, the event would be more traumatic when they move. Interestingly, a comparison study found more difficulty for military than for civilian youth who had left their old friends. Studies of adolescents native to Israel and of youth in Germany confirm American experiences. Again, the more psychopathological research has stressed the negative effects of relocation. However, past research has failed to reveal a significant relationship between emotional and behavioral problems and relocation among adolescents in the military community.

LIVING OVERSEAS

TOWARD the end of the Cold War, approximately 9 percent of enlisted soldiers and 31 percent of officers with more than fourteen years of service reported having moved with their spouse and/or children more than nine times. Commingled with

the mobile lifestyle are periodic moves to overseas military communities. Most soldiers complete
one tour overseas and elect to take their families
with them. The potential for stress and dysfunction is well documented as living overseas creates
its own special demands. Additional outcomes can
include separation from extended family, financial pressures, and education and career interrup-
tions. A review of some of the early studies
revealed that the negative impacts were more likely
to be compounded in already dysfunctional families. Other studies found particular negative outcomes facilitated by the host country's norms (e.g.,
permissive drinking norms for adolescents in Germany and heroin use in Thailand).

Although a considerable number of studies
emphasize the negative effects of living overseas,
more recent studies highlight the positive. Compared to their civilian peers, overseas American
students had college board scores above average
in many major testing areas. The most compre-
hensive study of military teenagers in Europe
found results contrary to the prevailing negative
perceptions of overseas living. For example, in
contrast to research focusing on culture shock (in
which individuals experience social maladjustment
when visiting or living in a society not their own)
and "stairwell syndrome" (a ramification of culture shock associated with the military, where
families isolate themselves and do not venture
outside the military community), it was discovered that over 95 percent of the teenagers sur-
veyed participated in at least one international
activity and that most had friends in their host
culture. Moreover, high school education overseas

was perceived by students and significant school faculty and staff to be equal to or better than that available in stateside schools. The learning of a second language also was a positive result of living overseas. That research also found that 34 percent of overseas teenagers could carry on a conversation in a foreign language and that most underestimated their competence after talking with the researcher. Another aspect of learning the language and protocol of the host country is an opportunity to take on new family roles by becoming the social liaison between one's family and the host culture, assisting with family activities like shopping, driving, and communicating in the foreign country.

The long-term effects of living overseas have received scant attention. One researcher concludes from her study that third culture kids require a period of adjustment to keep them moving toward developmental tasks of reachieving self-esteem, identity, intimacy, and a meaningful life—in essence, to reconstruct of their life to fit American cultural norms. Some researchers suggests that the "rootlessness" and "restlessness" of individuals reared in mobile families last long after those individuals have overtly adjusted to their return from overseas. What seems clear is that the experience is never lost.

TRANSITION TO CIVILIAN LIFE

THERE has been virtually no research on post-high school social behaviors and adjustment of military youth reared overseas. The exceptions are occupational linkage studies that have inconsistent results. Overall, early adult transition is a neglected research area. We know that the early stage of the life cycle is characterized by the central task of developing intimacy and beginning to make important life decisions, including marriage, career, religious values, and recreation activities. Intense cultural changes at this point can prove problematic.

For the military-reared young adult living in the United States, this stage of the life cycle may be accommodated more easily than for those living overseas. Young adults in overseas communities opting to forgo college may face a shortage of social supports and job opportunities. They also have a minority status in that most Americans their age are either soldiers or have recently married a soldier. Mary Tyler pointed to a small group of non-stateside college-bound teenagers who remain in Europe with parents after high school graduation. They tend to lack a stateside social network to assist them in relocating to the United States. Although some priority jobs go to members of military families in and around military bases, and university-level courses are available (e.g., the University of Maryland administers a European Division with campuses in Schwabisch Gmund and Mannheim, Germany, and night courses on most military bases throughout the world), many high school graduates postpone returning to the States until their parents do. A consequence may be the delay of transition to adulthood for mobile youth, for whom transition might be especially difficult, and an overdependency on family for all types of support can develop.

Finally, research on the long-term social-psychological implications of growing up in the context of an organization like the military is sparse. The remainder of this chapter focuses on the general sociological, historical, and psychological dimensions relevant to a unique group—a sample of adults raised as children, adolescents, and/or youth in mostly military and some other organization families between 1945 and 1990—the Cold War period—who share some primary education experiences overseas. My research explores some long-term implications of the demands of the military lifestyle on these individuals.

Participants, Measures, and Procedures

I have been surveying adult children from military and other organization families since 1991. To date, more than 260 participants have completed and returned the survey. Participants have included graduate and undergraduate students enrolled at major universities, adult participants at high school reunions, and respondents to an electronic call for volunteers via the Internet, electronic bulletin boards, and discussion lists.

More than three-fourths (78 percent) of the sample come from military families in which one parent was either an officer (43 percent) or an enlisted soldier (31 percent). Three-quarters of the sample had a parent who served in World War II, Korea, or Vietnam. Nine percent had parents who served in all three wars ($n = 26$). Seventy-nine percent have one, two, or three siblings. The vast majority of the sample reported having lived overseas for at least one year (97 percent), and 80 percent claimed to speak or have spoken at least one foreign language. Fifty-two different countries from around the planet are represented in the sample. The majority of the respondents speak European languages (85 percent), but other languages are represented, including Farsi and Swahili. More than half reported mingling with the local population often, very often, or totally. Many continue to travel outside the United States one or more times per year (49 percent).

More women than men have responded to the survey. The ages of the respondents range from eighteen to sixty-two. Whites (89 percent) are overrepresented and African (4.3 percent), Hispanic (.8 percent), Asian (1.6 percent), and biracial (1.6 percent) Americans are underrepresented relative to their proportions in the larger society. Just over half of the respondents are married (57 percent) and have one or more children (56 percent). Fourteen percent of the married respondents have a spouse from a similar background. The respondents are highly educated—96 percent indicate at least some college, and 30 percent possess an advanced degree. Most respondents currently reside in the United States (98 percent), and others live in the Caribbean, Europe, and Africa. Virginia (18 percent), Maryland (14 percent), Texas (10 percent), California (7 percent), Florida

(6 percent), Georgia (5 percent), and Colorado (4 percent) are the states most represented. Most respondents live either in a suburban area near a large city (31 percent) or in a large urban area (30 percent).

Occupationally, most respondents are either professionals (37 percent), in business management (14 percent), or students (13 percent). In terms of military service, 24 percent of the sample either has served in the military (21 percent) or is currently serving (3 percent). Of those with military experience, most were enlisted soldiers (64 percent), served in the Army (44 percent) or Air Force (39 percent), and served for four years or less (61 percent). Of those who never served, most said they had "no interest" (30 percent) or that "gender issues" (15 percent) were the reason for not joining. Political orientations are equally distributed on a five-point scale from very conservative (5 percent) to very liberal (13 percent).

Respondents received a survey and a self-addressed stamped envelope. The survey includes both forced-response questions and opportunities to elaborate on their experiences. One item (see Table 1) deals with the stresses of the military lifestyle—parental shift work, residence in foreign countries, risk of death or injury, geographic mobility, separations, normative constraints. Other stresses are caused by being personally anti-military, being part of a masculine-dominated culture and structure, and having to make transitions to civilian life. The possible scores range from one ("1") for *NOT AT ALL* to six ("6") for *EXTREMELY.*

Table 1
Military Lifestyle Stress Inventory

Looking back on growing up overseas for a period, please indicate the STRESS level you experienced with the following demands of the lifestyle:

Extremely
Quite a Bit
Moderately
A Little Bit
Slightly
Not at All

Father or mother working late or on shift work	OOOOOO
Living in a foreign country	OOOOOO
The risk of father or mother being injured or killed in military	OOOOOO
The periodic moves to different places	OOOOOO
Father or mother going away for extended periods of time	OOOOOO
The pressure not to get into trouble or it would affect parents' career	OOOOOO
Being personally anti-military	OOOOOO
The emphasis on being "macho" in and around the military	OOOOOO
Losing military privileges and becoming a "civilian"	OOOOOO
Other (specify) _____	OOOOOO
Other (specify) _____	OOOOOO

A Profile: Adult Children from Military and Other Organization Families

Figure 1 shows the percentage of respondents reporting that the demands of the military lifestyle were "Not at All" stressful. Twenty percent indicated that geographic mobility was not at all stressful, compared to 35 percent for separations, 31 percent for normative constraints, 82 percent for anti-military, 80 percent for masculine-dominated culture, 48 percent for transition to civilian life, 69 percent for shift work, 49 percent for foreign residence, and 53 percent for death or injury. Another way to interpret the chart is that geographic mobility, normative constraints (i.e., the pressures of rules and regulations imposed on the family by the organization), and separations are more stressful than other demands of military life.

The participants in the study also had an opportunity to respond in their own writing to two

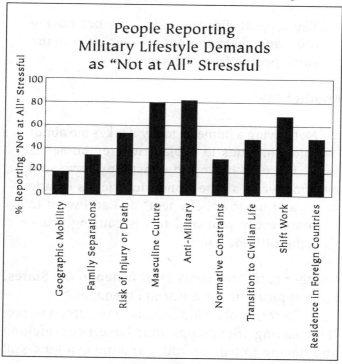

Figure 1

specific questions—What was the greatest disadvantage of the lifestyle? and What was the
greatest advantage of the lifestyle? Clearly the
greatest disadvantage, both in Figure 1 and in
their comments, was geographic mobility. Constantly moving throughout one's life imposed
three major disadvantages: feelings of rootlessness, losing friends, and rarely seeing members
of one's extended family. The effects of these disadvantages appear to remain with those raised
in military families for some time after they reach
adulthood. In terms of lacking roots, one person
told us,

> The biggest disadvantage ... is not having
> roots anywhere and not growing up with the
> same people from the same town.

Another said,

> Not having a home ... today it takes me about
> thirty minutes to explain where "home" is
> ... but also having to constantly have said
> goodbye to all the wonderful friends I made
> ... and having "itchy feet" as I still want to
> move every year and this is causing prob-
> lems with my career.

Another said, "No roots established in the States,
not a typical life for a normal teenager."
    In terms of losing friends, one person wrote,
"Not having friendships that have been lifelong
and having to tear up roots and move a lot." Still
another said,

> [It] is very stressful just picking up and moving every few years. One can fall out of touch with friends and extended family.

Another person wrote,

> There were times as a teenager that I felt I was simply 'missing out' by being away from other family members, grandmother, my cousins, and others.

One person pointed out that moving became more difficult with age:

> Saying goodbye to friends and memories [is a disadvantage of the lifestyle]. This should be self-explanatory and it is especially difficult the older one became.

Finally, one person confided an experience that can last a lifetime:

> The biggest disadvantage of moving and living overseas was being away from our family in the States. Our holidays, while fun, had something missing. My grandfather died while we were overseas and that was very hard on us.

While only a handful of people mentioned the disadvantages of the normative constraints of the military lifestyle in their written comments, almost all mentioned the wonderful opportunities of residing in a foreign country. Many viewed their overseas living as a profound developmental experience that they are very grateful to have had. Indeed, many of these reflections go to the heart of American democratic ideals—pluralism, diversity, and tolerance. One former Army dependent and Air Force veteran said:

> [While living overseas] I had limited contact with other Americans but gained great insight seeing how foreign nationals live, feel, and think. I think it makes one more objective and better able to deal with the pluses and minuses of being an American, and living in the USA. Our way may not always be the best way. I would *never* surrender my U.S. citizenship, but I have an appreciation for foreign values, customs, ideals, and history that I gained from my experiences in Europe and could easily live there.

Another said:

> Living overseas and being exposed to different cultures matured me faster and gave me greater understanding and tolerance for people. I think you mature faster as you have more experiences than if you were to stay your whole life in the States ... meet and deal with more people, travel on your own, etc. I just felt when I came back [to the States] that I knew and had experienced so much more than most of my U.S. peers.

Another said, "It made me adaptable to change, flexible, socially comfortable with people

[and] with diversity," while another said, "[It gave me] an opportunity to see other cultures." Another emphasized flexibility:

> Seems new places and cultures and getting to live in and among [other peoples was the greatest advantage]. We lived on the economy in Belgium and it was a wonderful experience for me. Getting to know a different country and its people so intimately made me a better person.

Conclusions

Many adults came of age in military and other organization families during the Cold War. In the popular culture, the negative stigma of *military brat* attempts to characterize their experience. Behavioral scientists are split on the effects of the military lifestyle on children, with most emphasizing the disadvantages. Increasingly, however, they are identifying the advantages.

In this chapter I have discussed a unique group—an availability sample of adults raised as children, adolescents, and/or youth in military and other organization families between 1945 and 1990, who share some primary education experience overseas and are now adults ($n = 258$). I have tried to frame the study, and ultimately the experiences of the respondents, within a military work and family perspective and describe the long-term implications of the demands of the military lifestyle.

White, urban, educated, and professional people are obviously overrepresented in the sample. However, the self-reports of the stress caused by family separation and geographic mobility are consistent with what researchers know about children and adolescents. The data reported here are also consistent with other findings on transitions to civilian life. One contradictory finding is the advantage of foreign residence. The one unexpected finding is how serious normative constraints were when these individuals were growing up. Researchers generally neglect this demand of the lifestyle.

The often-recurring cycle of parental departure, interim absence, and reunion is a social reality for military families. Separation was found to be the third most stressful demand of growing up in an organization. This result is especially telling given that approximately 75 percent of the sample had parents who had served in one or more wars.

Geographic mobility for military personnel was a common occurrence during the Cold War. Most of the literature shows inconsistent findings for children; however, the literature is clear for adolescents—relocation is a very stressful experience for adolescents in the military community. Again, the adolescent period of development is characterized by dissociating oneself from childhood yearnings and increasing cognitive development through an exploration of social, interpersonal, and intimate relationships with peers. A disruption during this developmental stage can be traumatic for adolescents, especially females. The results reported here are in the direction we would expect given what is known about military children. Most important, it appears that many years later, geographic mobility remains the most stressful demand of growing up in a military family.

In terms of organizational policies, two recommendations can be put forth. First, the military has usually relocated its members during the summer months, the thinking being that summer school vacation months coming between grades are the best times to relocate. Recently, however, Mary Tyler noted that mobility during the school year is *less* traumatic than during the summer months because school-age children and youth could more easily and quickly assimilate into a new peer group.

Second, although residence in a foreign country interacts with relocation, this demand was not reported to be as stressful as other demands. These results are also consistent with recent studies of foreign residence. A review of the early literature revealed that the negative impacts were likely to be compounded in already dysfunctional families. More recent studies have emerged that are highlighting positive features of living overseas and include positive educational and cross-cultural experiences, second language acquisition, and the opportunity to assert new family roles by becoming the social liaison between family and host culture (e.g., assisting parents with activities like shopping, driving, and communicating in the foreign country). In addition, the people completing the surveys told us that although they felt out

of touch for awhile, in terms of the popular culture (e.g., music, television, clothing styles), the
benefits of having lived overseas are, in the long
run, much more meaningful and fulfilling.

   After high school, young adults in military
families must transition out of the organization,
either to college or the work force. This stage of the
life cycle is characterized by developing intimacy
and making decisions about such life elements as
marriage, career, religious values, and recreation
activities. The lack of a "civilian" social network
forces many to postpone this period for awhile and
remain in their parents' home. This finding may also
explain why children of soldiers often grow up to
become soldiers or marry them.

   Finally, organizations, especially the military, Foreign Service, and religious affiliates, exercise direct constraints and normative pressure
on their members and indirect constraints on family members through the service member. Behavior can be both prescriptive and proscriptive.
There is no literature explaining the relationship
between or impact of normative organization constraints on children, adolescents, and youth. The
high stress responses reported here suggest that
this may be a salient feature for those growing up
in the military and other organization contexts,
especially in relation to the most salient demand
of the lifestyle—geographic mobility. Most important, it is very obvious that some essential individual, interpersonal, and social skills are gained
from living abroad that are easily recognizable to
and valued by employers. These skills include tolerance, flexibility, multilingualism, and travel

savvy—characteristics not always obvious from a résumé. These skills are very important in an increasingly diverse and internationally oriented world and are generally found wanting among the majority of Americans. The internationally or multiculturally minded employer could profit from the intuitive social skills of geographically mobile and overseas-experienced adults. Perhaps the most important finding is that the work and family context that we are raised in needs much more exploration. This study only begins to scratch the proverbial surface. The experiences of Cold War children should not be ignored, as they may indeed be the pioneers of an international citizenry.

Works Cited

Alsikafi, M., Gerald Globetti, and E. G. Christy (1979). "Abusive alcohol drinking: A study of social attitudes of youth in a military community." *Drug Forum, 7*(3 & 4), pp. 317–328.

Bowen, Gary L. (1986). "Intergenerational occupational inheritance in the military: A reexamination." *Adolescence, 21,* pp. 623–629.

Carlsmith, Lyn (1973). "Some personality characteristics of boys separated from their fathers during world war II." *Ethos,* pp. 467–477.

Cottrell, Ann Baker, and Ruth Hill Useem (1994). "ATCKs Maintain Global Dimensions Throughout Their Lives." *NewsLinks* (International Schools Services), pp. 13–15, 30.

Erikson, Erik (1950). *Childhood and Society.* (New York: W.W. Norton).

Faris, John H. (1981). "The all-volunteer force: Recruitment from military families." *Armed Forces and Society*, 7, pp. 545–559.

Gonzalez, Victor (1970). *Psychiatry and the Army Brat*. (Springfield, IL: C.C. Thomas).

The Great Santini (1984), A Warner Bros./Orion Pictures Release. Produced by Charles A. Pratt. Written for the screen and directed by Lewis John Carlino. Burbank, CA: Warner Home Video.

Grubbs, Jim (1988). *APO San Francisco 96525: Growing Up in the Military*. (Springfield, IL: Independent Publishing).

Hormuth, Stefan E. (1990). *The Ecology of the Self: Relocation and Self Concept Change*. (Cambridge, England: Cambridge University Press).

Hunter, Edna J. (1982). *Families Under the Flag: A Review of Military Family Literature*. (New York: Praeger).

Hunter, Edna J., and D. Stephen Nice (1978) (Eds.). *Children of Military Families: A Part Yet Apart*. (Washington, DC: U.S. Government Printing Office).

Jensen, Peter S., R. L. Lewis, and S. N. Xenakis (1986). "The military family in review: Context, risk and prevention." *Journal of the American Academy of Child Psychiatry*, 25, pp. 225–234.

Kojak, George J. (1974). "American community in Bangkok, Thailand: A model of social disintegration." *American Journal of Psychiatry*, 131(11), pp. 1229–1233.

LaGrone, D. A. (1978). "The military family syndrome." *American Journal of Psychiatry*, 135, pp. 1040–1043.

Mayer, Christine M. (1995). *There's No Place Like ... Home?: The Importance of Regional Identity with Former Military Dependents*. Paper presented at the Eastern Sociological Society Meetings, Philadelphia, PA, March/April.

McCluskey, Karen Curnow (Ed.). (1994). *Notes from a Traveling Childhood: Readings for Internationally Mobile Parents & Children.* (Washington, DC: Foreign Service Youth Foundation).

Orthner, Dennis K., Martha M. Giddings, and William H. Quinn (1989). "Growing up in an organization family." In Gary L. Bowen and Dennis K. Orthner (Eds.), *The Organization Family: Work and Family Linkages in the U.S. Military,* pp. 117–142. (New Yrok: Praeger).

Paden, Lindsay B., and Laurence J. Pezor (1993). "Uniforms and youth: The military child and his or her family." In Florence W. Kaslow (Ed.), *The Military Family in Peace and War,* pp. 3–24. (New York: Springer).

Pederson, Frank A. (1966). "Relationships between father absence and emotional disturbance in male military dependents." *Merrill-Palmer Quarterly, 12,* pp. 321–331.

Raviv, Amarim, Giora Keinan, Yehuda Abazon, and Alona Raviv (1990). "Moving as a stressful life event for adolescents." *Journal of Community Psychology, 18,* pp. 130–140.

Salmon, Joy L. (1988). *The Relationship of Stress and Mobility to the Psychosocial Development and Well-being of Third-Culture-Reared Early Adults.* Unpublished doctoral dissertation, University of Florida.

Segal, Mady Wechsler (1989). "The nature of work and family linkages: A theoretical perspective." In Gary L. Orthner and Dennis K. Bowen (Eds.), *The Organization Family: Work and Family Linkages in the U.S. Military,* pp. 3–36 (New York: Praeger).

Shaw, Jon A. (1987). "Children in the military." *Psychiatric Annals, 17,* 539–544.

Smith, William J. (1980) *Army Brat: A Memoir.* (New York: Persea Books).

Terr, L. C. (Ed.) (1992). "Debate forum: 'Resolved: Military family life is hazardous to the mental health of children.'" *Journal of the American Academy of Child and Adolescent Psychiatry, 31* (5), (September), pp. 984–987.

Thomas, George W. (1984). "Military parental effects and career orientation under the AVF: Enlisted personnel." *Armed Forces and Society, 10,* pp. 293–310.

Truscott, Mary R. (1990). *Brats: Children of the Military Speak Out.* (New York: E.P. Dutton).

Tuttle, William M., Jr., (1993). *"Daddy's Gone to War": The Second World War in the Lives of America's Children.* (New York: Oxford University Press).

Tyler, Mary P. (1987). *The Teenager in Europe.* (United States Army Medical ResearchUnit—Europe, HQ, 7th Medical Command).

Wertsch, Mary E. (1996). *Military Brats: Legacies of Childhood Inside the Fortress* (Bayside, NY: Aletheia).

Wolf, Charlotte (1969). *Garrison Community: A Study of an Overseas American Military Colony.* (Westport, CT: Greenwood).

BEHIND THE SWINGING DOOR
Jody Merrill-Foster

JODY MERRILL-FOSTER went overseas for the first time in 1962, when her husband joined the U.S. Information Service and was sent to Athens as a radio specialist. Over the next twenty-three years they and their three children lived in a variety of posts, including Tehran, Kabul, Accra, New Delhi, Amman, Manila, and Durban. Now retired, they live in the White Mountains of New Hampshire, where she writes poetry and articles and does occasional radio commentaries.

IT HAD ALL SEEMED quite straightforward that hot day in July when we first learned that we would be moving overseas. My husband had called from Washington with the news of our assignment, our very first trip outside the United States. That afternoon a neighbor dropped in for coffee. I told her the exciting news. "We're going to Athens!" "That's *great!*" she replied. "You'll be so much nearer to Bangor!"

For our three small children, moving abroad was no stranger than moving from Ohio to New Hampshire. But to us it seemed the start of a great adventure. It never occurred to us then that, down the line, this experience would change our lives, but in very different ways. Our attitudes and behavior would thereafter always reflect the people we had known and the things we had seen during those years. We adults would become perhaps more selective, more sensitive, more discriminating, but we would remain what we had always been—Americans. Our children, though, would become no longer solely American but, rather, members of a larger world family, connected in a way that we could never be. Perhaps it is what Tennyson meant when he wrote that he was "a part of all that he had seen."

Adults leave America for the first time with a clearly defined sense of place. They are "Americans," and often that sense of identity—of association with place—becomes a yardstick by which they measure subsequent, wider experience. But children assimilate new languages, cultures, scenery, and people quite naturally and without distinction.

This became clear one day when our fourth-grader came home from the international school in Tehran and asked, "Mom, where's my home?" In geography class the students had been asked to identify their hometown. Our son had responded that his "home" was the small apartment in Tehran where he lived with his dad, his mother, and his siblings. When the teacher continued to ask where he was "from," he was stumped. Home leaves were spent in his grandparents' small apartment in New York or in his other grandparents' big old house in New Hampshire. He had no idea at all how to answer the question.

There came a day when Dad came home for lunch in Afghanistan, bringing the news that he was going to be assigned to Saigon. "It's an unaccompanied tour, Hon'. No wives can go. You'll have a choice. You can go to Baguio in the Philippines or Bangkok. Or you can go home and be near your folks." After much mulling, the decision was made to go back to New England. Being near the children's beloved Grandpa might assuage the difficulties of being without Dad.

But even that decision was not wholly satisfactory. It was 1967. Students at Dartmouth had tried to burn the ROTC building, and feelings for and against our involvement in Vietnam ran high. Our two sons entered the local public school, where they found to their dismay that their father's involvement in the war made them fair game, the butt of cruel jokes and victims of the kind of locker-room hazing that brought them home with torn underwear from being swung by their waistbands by bigger boys. They were "the new kids" transferred from some weird place no one had ever heard of, and—worst of all—their dad worked for the "enemy," the government.

Beyond the absence of their father, beyond the nightly news from Vietnam, the children fought the daily challenge of trying to gain acceptance at their new school. Years later, in letters, both confessed that those years had been the most miserable of their lives. They never really felt accepted, and it was with great relief that they returned to their "real lives," our next assignment overseas.

This dichotomy again became painfully clear years later, when our daughter decided to write her master's thesis in journalism on what she had learned were called TCKs. In her thesis she recounted how, when she was twelve, she'd been called to the principal's office at a small school in Ghana and told that she was to leave school and go right home. Her grandmother had had a heart attack in New York, and the family would be returning immediately to the United States. She wrote, "I went home and helped my mother pack. That night we were on a plane. I never saw my house again. I never saw my room. I never said goodbye to my best friend." In her mind, she was not "going home." She was "leaving home."

I remember that day well. Despite our grave concern about Grandmother, I couldn't help an underlying excitement that I would soon see my parents, that New York would probably be covered with snow, that I would drink cold water right out of the tap without having to boil it first, and that with Christmas only a month away I could take the children window-shopping on Fifth Avenue. This Ghanaian house was the place where I had been living, but the place I was going to was "home."

For the most part, the children ingested these new experiences with enthusiasm. In Athens, they were introduced to the biggest pistachio nuts they'd ever seen, doled out one by one as rewards for learning to count in Greek. They learned to sing Greek folk songs, to understand the history of the Acropolis and the Parthenon; they learned about Lord Byron from seeing his name carved on a pillar at Sounion. They learned to love Greek food and to adjust to the Greek schedule of siestas and dining at ten. But they also learned to share the Greek gift of laughter, of history, and they became the beneficiaries of the Greek love of children. On the island of Tinos, visiting a Greek family, they were awakened at five to accompany the son of their hosts, a priest, as he walked to the neighboring villages to say Mass. They were given the "honor" of ringing the church bell to summon the faithful to the church. In later years, when Greece and Turkey planted competing flags on an Aegean island, they understood what the issue meant and what the rivalry was all about.

In Iran, they were introduced to monarchy and learned to respect the dignity and devotion of Islam. They watched their neighbors observing the fast of Ramadan, the celebration of Eid al Fitr; they saw simple working men stop in the dusty roads to wash face, hands, head, and feet, then kneel by the roadside in noon prayer. As they grew older and saw the rise of Islamic fundamentalism in Libya, Egypt, and Algeria, they remembered those workmen. They understood the passion.

The Armenian minority in Iran taught them something of history. Later, when the Soviet Union imploded and dissension reemerged in Azerbaijan, they understood where the Armenian position was grounded.

Alexander the Great and Genghis Khan entered their lives in Afghanistan. There they learned that Islam had mystics of its own, whose writings were older than those of Christianity. They visited the wastelands above Bamian where Genghis Khan had vowed to "destroy every living thing." They made friends with the children of Istalif and visited the parents of those children as they wove their legendary rugs. One day an American woman tried to bargain with a rug maker. He replied with great dignity, "Memsahib, that is the only rug I've ever made. It is my life's work." Out of their experience with machine-made American goods, the children learned to gauge value in a new way.

The absorptive capacity of Indian culture through centuries of invasions, repelled and accommodated, taught them to respect a history older than their own. In New Delhi, they joined in Diwali celebrations and gave *raki* ribbons to their close friends. Some of their school friends studied the myriad forms of Indian dance that have been performed in the same way over generations. One year, the oldest made the trip by third-class train from Delhi north to the mouth of the Ganges. There he surreptitiously lowered a small bottle into the water to obtain a sample of the water, believed to contain restorative, absolving power. Like a typical schoolboy, he wanted to take it back to the lab and run it through a test tube.

All three children rode the train to Agra, leaning out of the windows to buy cardamom-flavored tea from platform vendors and sharing snacks with fellow passengers. At the Taj Mahal, they stood silent before its ethereal beauty. The middle child closed his eyes and walked backwards to the edge of the reflecting pool fronting the palace. There, turning slowly around, he opened his eyes, drew a sharp breath, and sighed, "Mom! It's exactly the way I always thought it would be!"

When the oldest returned to the United States as a junior in high school he began to confront the difficulties of fitting in. In the school debating society, he discovered that his instinctive view of any question of international affairs was invariably different from that of the other debaters. Whereas they tended to support all American positions, he often saw a second side to the issue. While other students avidly followed football and baseball scores, he—having been brought up on soccer—often found himself ignorant of stats and players, to the disbelief of his friends.

The laundromat was a major obstacle. His experience of laundry had been the twice-weekly dhobi who did the family wash in the bathtub and hung it in the sun to dry. The complexities of wash cycles were quite beyond him for most of his first term. The Coke machine in the school lounge mesmerized him. He was amazed at the way the cans were automatically replaced after each purchase. Coke, in his experience, came in chipped brown bottles, delivered by the case. Often, he found himself alone in the student lounge when the evening television news began. Conversation in the dorm seldom included anything about the world outside. He felt himself drawn to the foreign students, choosing to sit with them at meals. He just felt awkward—an outsider.

The second child left home a little later, transiting Ivory Coast and Paris en route to boarding school in New Hampshire. This boy, who was quite able to navigate rickshaws in Singapore and pedicabs in Delhi, found himself confounded by the New York cabby. He was driven all over Long Island at a cost of $20 on what should have been a ten-minute drive from La Guardia to Queens. Though his school was rather unique and small, his sense of displacement was acute.

Those were turbulent years. Antiwar demonstrations by Vietnam vets, the court-martial of William Calley for the massacre at My Lai, the emergence of the new nation of Bangladesh, lowering of the voting age, publication of the Pentagon Papers, and the admission of China to the United Nations all conspired to focus the attention of American teens on the world outside. Yet in his small New England school he found that few of his fellow students had any interest in these events. Fresh from Africa, he was surrounded by white faces. He missed the comradeship of the night watchmen with whom, sneaking out of the house at night, he had played the African stone game, *awari*, chewed cola nuts, and tried to learn Fulani.

To adults, reentry after twenty-three years overseas brought several major challenges. Perhaps one tends to idealize one's own country when one is absent from it. We found ourselves astounded and somewhat depressed by the waste we saw all about us, the "planned obsolescence" built into the economy. We were introduced to a world of plastic credit. Friends, returning from Europe, tried to pay cash for a rental car in New York and were denied when they were unable to produce any credit cards. Used as we were to paying cash, we had to learn a whole new way of thinking about money.

The casual use (and misuse) of American abundance shocked us. Once you have walked the streets of Bombay, followed for blocks by scrawny urchins begging for food, you look at poverty in a new way. Once you have seen the squatter children in Pampanga, the Philippines, scrambling over "Smoky Mountain," the burning garbage dump outside the American military base, in hopes of a bit of fruit or rice, you are never again free of those images in your mind's eye. So in America, seeing uneaten rolls being removed from your table at a restaurant and knowing that American law requires that they be discarded, you can't help but remember. You think of Mother Teresa's sisters picking up unused airline meals and leftover dishes from hotels for their soup kitchen in Calcutta, and you can't forget. You feel the same helplessness you used to feel as a child when your mother said, "Now, eat your spinach. Just think of the starving Armenians!" And you remember how you used to mutter to yourself, under your breath, "Well give it to *them* then!" But you know those hungry children can't have the rolls, the butter, or the large piece of uneaten meat left by a diner at an adjoining table. And you're angry. You're ashamed to have so much when you remember what a little bit meant to children you have known.

The returnee finds himself reassessing his country and its citizens in light of the views he's heard expressed abroad. Once, in South Africa, an English-born South African told us, "You can always tell the Americans. They talk louder than anybody else. They are always convinced that their idea is the best one, their solution the only reasonable one, and they don't like to listen." That characterization stung. And yet, on a street in Paris, I heard an American repeating, louder and louder, the same phrase in English in the vain (and rather arrogant) expectation that his listener would finally "get it."

After all our opportunities to learn, we now cringe when we hear public figures constantly refer to the United States in smug, self-congratulatory terms, particularly in the presence of representatives of other nations. It suddenly seems like a kind of national bad manners. We are appalled at events such as the rape trial in Okinawa, and we realize how fragile are the relations between nations, so painstakingly built and so easily rent by the mindless behavior of three individuals.

We once heard a Filipina remark that Americans seemed to be such friendly people but that that impression had no reality. Since reentry, we have had many experiences that confirm her feelings. Except for those in small towns, Americans do not seem to the returning expatriate particularly friendly. In comparison with Africans, Asians, and Middle Easterners, who invariably want to know all about you, Americans at home often indicate a complete lack of interest in other Americans, let alone in foreigners. It made us sad to walk into the cafeteria of a major college and see the foreign students dining together with not a single American among them. As an American abroad, you realize you were never so ostracized.

Adjustment to the violence and vulgarity of American films and television is difficult for us. Americans' preoccupation with themselves and with the more bizarre events of their public life is almost embarrassing to the returnee. A house guest of ours, a supreme court judge from

Taiwan, happened to be with us the day that O.J. Simpson's Bronco rode the California freeway. The ride absorbed all three network evening news shows for what seemed like an eternity. In the understatement of the year, our guest observed that he wished there were some channel to which we might turn where we could find out whether anything "important" had happened in the world that day. As I recall, there were massive massacres in Rwanda going on at that time. Our narcissistic contemplation of our own national aberrations was quite beyond his comprehension.

We feel uncomfortable at negative campaigning, at targeted negative advertising in which one product denigrates another by name. These "jugular ads" are illegal in some European countries and do not redound to our credit, indicating, as they do, that nastiness pays. Other cultures emphasize civility so much, the returnee finds the almost universal rudeness in America discomfiting. Events like the summer baseball strike are almost incomprehensible when you've been away so long. In the places we've lived, annual salaries are counted in the hundreds of dollars. When you start talking about millions for putting a ball through a hoop, or multimillions for owning a team, such salaries become impossible to assimilate. These are the kinds of reentry difficulties we find as adults.

I've asked fellow returnees what they most enjoy and admire about the America they come back to. Always, high up on the list are fine daily papers, wonderful supermarkets, the multiplicity of choices of brands and quality in this country.

The creature comforts of endless hot water simply by turning a handle, the relative cheapness of
food and fuel—all of these rate high. Opportunities for motivated individuals to set goals and at-
tain them are impressive. In short, life for
Americans is for the most part comfortable and
pleasant. While we are aware of much that is ve-
nal, silly, and adolescent in American life, we agree
that there is much to admire.

For young people, however, the reentry
hurdles are less specific than for their parents. In
his or her own way, each of our three children
experienced something of the feeling of being an
outsider. Our eldest, immediately on entering university, volunteered to work with foreign students,
holding orientations and helping them get settled.
He majored in Chinese and now works in the field
of cross-cultural training with Asian governments
and businesses. The second entered the Air Force
and served overseas. An African-American col-
league with whom he worked used to tease him,
saying, "Man, you're a black man in a white skin!"
The third child found her niche in journalism, traveling continually in Europe, Southeast Asia, and
the Caribbean. She once phoned us from an airport and commented, "You know, Mom, it's really funny. When I'm in America, I always feel
vaguely depressed, like I don't belong! But the
minute I'm on a plane going somewhere, then
suddenly—I'm me again!"

I think often of an Afghan professor we
knew. He always showed up for our lessons in Farsi
looking like something out of a British Bond Street
ad—suit sharply pressed, shoes reflecting his face,

hair perfectly combed, hands and nails immaculate. He confessed to us one day that, in his home, there was no hot water.

I thought of him the other day when I saw a middle-aged woman walking from the supermarket to her Cadillac. Her hair was bleached blonde, her general appearance le dernier cri. She wore a pair of stone-washed, bleached blue jeans with asymmetrical tears in both knees and across the back of one thigh. And I thought of Selindile in South Africa. She used to arrive for work wearing a plum-colored suit with matching felt hat, cast-offs of the elegant lady for whom her mother worked. She often arrived late because her bus—in those last-gasp days of apartheid—had been stopped as it was leaving the black area where she lived so that the police could check the passengers' "domb passes," the papers without which blacks couldn't enter the white areas. Selindile would rush in, apologize for being tardy, go to her room, and emerge a few minutes later wearing her checked cotton "uniform."

I felt angry, seeing the woman in the deliberately torn jeans. It seemed, after all the poverty I'd seen, simple arrogance. A comment our middle son had once made came to mind: "Mom, when I went to India I learned what real poverty was. It was a shoemaker, riding eight miles to his home after dark with no light on his bicycle. But here in America, poverty means having only one car in your garage and one VCR in your livingroom."

When the children were young and returned to America, they felt diminished because they didn't know the things all their peers knew. Now, as young adults, they are beginning to understand. Their experiences were not deprivations but enlargements. They were being readied for life in Marshall McLuhan's global village—the world John Donne meant when he wrote that "no man is an island." They believe that all our lives are inextricably connected to one another and that together we are, in truth, the Family of Man.

Rolling Stones Smooth Out Nicely
Linda Bell

LINDA BELL *is an editor, interviewer, and researcher on cross-cultural topics. During 1991 and 1992 she served as interviewer and transcriber for the Foreign Service Spouses Oral History Project, which was published in* Married to the Foreign Service *(Twayne, 1993). This selection is excerpted from her book* Hidden Immigrants: Legacies of Growing Up Abroad, *which was published by Cross Cultural Publications in 1996.*

IT WAS WHEN MY four-year-old daughter, Amy, asked me what language they speak in the States that I realized I might be in over my head. We were about to leave French West Africa on home leave, and it was clear that she did not want to have to deal with yet another language. When she asked if everyone would understand her, I answered yes. But then I realized that by her very question they might not; maybe her language was the same, but not much else about her young life was recognizable to children her age in America, or even to our respective families.

Born overseas, taken already to three different foreign countries to live, she was a product
both of our American home and of the cultures in
which she had lived. What we meant and what
she meant by "home" were not the same. After
all, she was home, as far as she knew. Amy would,
from that very first home leave, be a cultural outsider in her own country of origin. Already she
was set apart by her experiences in ways I couldn't
begin to fathom. I could only try to understand
and, in turn, help her understand.

If our children weren't to have roots, I pon-
dered, at least they would have a world view. As a
mother I hoped our children could learn to accept
cultural diversity with compassion and use their
knowledge to make the world smaller, more com-
prehensible. I knew they would be different—there
was nothing I could do about that—but I also assumed that those differences could give them
something meaningful in return.

By contrast, my husband and I grew up in
the same small town, where we had "landed"
roots. I couldn't help wondering what would happen to these "unlanded" children? By default and
a little training I became an observer, an amateur
social scientist. One thing led to another, and when
I returned to the States after a "last" posting
abroad, I started to dig for some answers. The first
thing I found was that there wasn't much to be
found—very little written or documented, no studies, and perhaps just a bit of skepticism on the
part of otherwise reasonable career Foreign Service personnel about why there should be. They
said things like "Kids always adjust." My long ex-

perience overseas told me otherwise, but I was more interested in how the ups and downs played out in their adult lives. I wanted to know what kinds of things helped or hindered their adjustments along the way. I wanted to know if their childhood experiences influenced their adult choices in terms of their professions, their relationships. I wanted to know how they saw themselves within American culture.

In 1991 I started conducting oral interviews to this end. First I started talking to people I had known as children in our early overseas postings. From them, I got the names of others. I obtained many other leads by networking within the foreign service community. Sometimes I serendipitously met people who had grown up overseas, and I interviewed them. A few of the people I interviewed were self-selected through a notice I put in a newsletter.

My criteria were simple. I asked that either my informants themselves or their parents had lived overseas during most of their high school years, and I wanted lots of international mobility. Most of the respondents had lived in four to five countries during childhood. In all, I interviewed thirteen individuals, seven women and six men, ranging in age from twenty-eight to forty-two.

Mine is not a scientific survey; I am a journalist, not a social scientist. My intent is to lay the information out in good faith—the good news and the bad—and then see what insights evolve.

Out of the thirteen people I interviewed, only one had never married; one was divorced. Six had been married for more than ten years, suggesting an ability to sustain long-term relationships. Unlike what you'd expect, all but one of them had a stable, unchanging lifestyle. That's not to say that they don't change jobs or houses and travel often both domestically and overseas for business and pleasure, but that they've settled in one place either by accident or by design. For example, one man in his early forties, resident in Maryland since 1967, married to a woman he met in high school in England, and the father of four children, said, "I feel in constant transition. I'm stable, but I still feel like I'm always living out of a suitcase."

For my respondents, roots are defined in terms of people and not place, even if they've been in the same place for a long time. They made comments like these:

Now I define roots through connections and associations, shared experiences, shared backgrounds with people and places.... It's important that I know where old friends are, even though I might not make a conscious effort to contact them.... Don't ask me why this is so. But it is important to me that I know that if I need to get in touch with them, that person is there.

What every kid who grows up like I did knows is that "I was there, I did live there." Now it is difficult to reconnect with the people that know I was there, because they were there too. That's why the reunions are so important to me, so it won't seem all a dream and

> evaporate without any connection. It helps
> convince me in my own mind that I was there!
> It's a connection with the reality.

WHILE all but two of my informants rated their childhood experiences overseas very positively—even with the traumas of entry into America, recurrent losses, and exposure to political crisis and violence—certain manifestations of this legacy carry over even into mid-adulthood.

One issue is status. I don't mean the kind of status that comes of being the child of an ambassador or even the loss of the privileges and services some of these children come to expect. What is far more pervasive is their own definition of themselves as "different." As they move from one culture to another, their sense of being on the outside of that culture is the only thing that remains constant and defines them. They are used to being set apart by all those things that identify foreigners—their looks, their language, their clothes and customs, their habits and actions. They play baseball in Hyde Park and wear loafers to Asian bazaars. They team up together by language, not nationality. Affiliations to countries, religions, racial groupings, economic classes—identifiers that might mark them in their own culture—are lost to them. Instead it is their sense of being different and transient that binds them together.

Once the child accepts being or feeling different, buys into it, learns to take advantage of it, and accepts it as a definition of who they are,

they're often loath to shake off that definition later
in life. The following comments are typical:

> I like being the "different one." Even in this
> culture I am different. My husband gets mad
> at me. He says, "You always say you don't
> want to be conventional."

> Suddenly, when I got to college in Minne-
> sota, I realized no one knew who I was. In
> Bombay or Cairo, everybody knew who I
> was—some American.

> I've always been different. And I've always
> found pride in being different. Partly that's
> making the best of the situation, partly I
> think because I've always liked to stand out.

The obvious questions come to mind: How
do these global nomads continue to maintain their
status as "different" when they become adults
within their own culture? And if they do, can they
ever expect to be anything but marginal to it?

When they were first confronted with
American culture, as teenagers or in their early
twenties, my informants struggled between their
need to feel different and their need to fit in. Some
felt that they lost their integrity when they tried
too hard to conform:

> I do remember having this really serious
> sense of not being able to be who I really
> was. In fact, I still have these battles and

usually just revert to an "I'd rather not talk about it" stance.

When I was a youngster trying to cope with the traumas of moving around, the thing I remember trying to do consciously was fit in. What I've tried to do as an adult, consciously, is to draw lines to challenge, confront. It's exactly the opposite.

Others found it more natural to assert their marginality by wearing ethnic clothing, speaking with an accent, or hanging out with international friends and students. However they chose to see their way through this transitional phase, the results were often the same.

During their twenties, all of my informants returned overseas for various reasons and for varying lengths of time; four went into the Peace Corps; one was a Foreign Service officer; one is currently a Foreign Service spouse; two went on various academic scholarships; three lived or traveled frequently overseas on business; others have gone on frequent holidays. Many returned to some of the countries where they had lived as children. However, once on their own, in an adult role, they saw things much differently than they had as children. Sometimes the harsh realities clashed with the fantasies. As one man said,

I was very unhappy to leave London and did fly back the following Christmas.... I was there for three weeks. Then and there I realized it would never be the same. It was different. The fact that my parents weren't there, my home wasn't there—I was on my own and vulnerable. I either had to make it on my own, or leave.

As adults these individuals are not generally movers, shakers, or joiners in their communities. They prefer to watch from the sidelines. Many continue to cultivate their marginality—often unknowingly—in various ways: through their speech, habits and preferences, career choices, choice of spouse, or place of residence. For example, one man told me:

> Washington is a very odd sort of America. Particularly in D.C. As a white male, living in a city that is virtually segregated, where I could never expect to have real influence over political decision-making in this town, or run for political office or any of that, I'm like the expatriate again—the observer—living right there on the surface, but not responsible.

Of ten married respondents, seven are married to spouses who are either minorities, first-generation immigrants, military children, or children of cross-cultural couples. One man, who had asserted his militancy on the Palestinian issue all through college, said:

> I remember feeling a great deal of resentment and anger that I couldn't engage people on the importance of the Palestinian issue. By the time I met my wife, I was

already beginning to drift away from it.... In a way, meeting her allowed me to engage on it at a personal level. We had a lot in common as a result of her being Jewish.

As for the choice of a career, many of my informants continue to work overseas. In this way overseas Americans have fostered legions of sensitive government servants, businesspeople, development specialists, and academics. In my sample only two were working for corporate industries. The others were either self-employed, working in government, working in service industries, or employed by private nonprofit organizations. I had the feeling that they liked calling their own shots and helping people in their professional lives.

Another childhood legacy that all my informants said they were grateful for is their continuing ability to adapt. Often described as cultural chameleons, they quickly learn to take on the coloring and habits of the cultural norm, whatever that norm happens to be. I heard comments like the following:

Frankly, all the Foreign Service experience was valuable—like [the need to] adjust, the premium on figuring out someone else's culture, putting yourself in someone else's shoes, it's almost second nature to do that.

I have a conviction that I will always be comfortable out of my surroundings, or not feeling strange.

Learning to adapt quickly is usually a positive skill, a good defense against life's ups and downs. But it too can have a dark side. One thoughtful, introspective woman told me:

> The one thing I haven't really conquered has to do with the downside of the ability to adapt. I became aware that I was too good at adapting, that I could fit into any crowd very quickly and effectively, no matter what kind of a group it was. Privately I would hold back and have a lot of private judgments about it ... and after a while I began to realize that this was dishonest. For example, in a professional setting, rather than challenge, I became very skillful at figuring out how to advance my agenda using language and concepts they would respond to. To some extent that's a good thing to know. But after a certain point it becomes manipulative.... I've stated it at its most extreme. But I began to be aware at some point in my late twenties that I needed to be careful. I was too good at it.

In my conversations with these adults about their childhood overseas, they shared with me some of the things they felt passionate about—things that they felt really helped them adjust as they went along and others that they felt really hurt them.

Not unexpectedly, the more cross-cultural identity and emotional investment a person had in a place, the harder it was to leave, and the greater the need to grieve over the separation. On the other hand, the informants with the most cross-cultural exposure were the most comfortable with the experience as adults. They said over and over again that they wouldn't have had their childhood any other way, even with the pain of leaving places and finding that they had to adjust to their own culture.

By contrast, two respondents felt that they had been denied or had missed the cross-cultural experience, and their responses reflected their anger. One had lived in American compounds in the former Soviet Union and Europe, and the other had never been in one place long enough, owing to short or abbreviated tours and evacuations, to really get to know anything about where he was living. Upon returning to the United States, they felt that they had been deceived. Overseas they had felt completely American; upon returning they found, to their hurt and dismay, that they were not! And yet they had no knowledge and understanding of the other cultures, no growth through attachment, to balance their cultural deficiency.

Another aspect mentioned by almost all of my informants was self-determination. When families worked on transfer assignments together, even if the children knew that their own preferences might not pan out, they still needed to know that they were being included. Of course, it didn't always work out that way. Several of my informants were evacuated out of places very quickly. Others were told about an impending move only a few weeks in advance. Sometimes that was their parents' choice; other times it was simply a result of the vagaries of the system. The adults I talked to were comforted when pets could accompany them to the next posting. They were much more ambivalent about child-minders and domestic helpers. One angry man told me how his parents had sold almost all of their belongings every time they moved. He had never felt that he could hold on to anything and had lacked a sense of continuity. I interviewed two siblings who had had an easier than usual passage into American culture even though they were in boarding schools overseas from very early ages and didn't live in America until one was entering college and the other was in his last year of high school. One reason for this, they said, was their strong identification with their grandmother and her home, which had been in the family for many years. They had enjoyed extended summer holidays there almost annually with cousins, aunts, and uncles, as well as with their own parents when possible. They were the only two I interviewed who showed no hesitation in answering the question, "Where are you from?"

And lastly there was a definite correlation between how well a child got along in any one place and how well the parents liked it and liked what they were doing in general.

As for my daughter Amy, now in her mid-twenties, I guess my own hopes for her to be more tolerant, more open to the world, are being realized as she enters into a marriage with an African Ph.D. candidate from South Africa. We reap what we sow!

Phoenix Rising:
A Question of Cultural Identity*
Barbara F. Schaetti

BARBARA SCHAETTI, M.S., is a second-generation American-Swiss global nomad and president of Transition Dynamics, Inc. (based in Seattle). She consults and trains on global nomad issues around the world, served on the board of directors of Global Nomads International from 1991 to 1996, and was recently elected a founding member of GNI's advisory board.

IT WAS A BEAUTIFUL spring Sunday in Switzerland. My aunt, uncle, a cousin, and I were on a "wanderweg," following one of the many walking paths that weave through the Swiss countryside. We roamed through forests, passed vistas sweeping toward the Alps, meandered through farm villages. I felt at ease, familiar in the memories of many other such walks from both my childhood and more recent years. We stopped for a moment to greet other walkers on the trail. My aunt introduced me as her "American niece." I felt my body stop. I wanted to cry out, "No!"

*This article originally appeared in the Spring/Summer 1996 issue of *Global Nomad Perspectives*.

Why? I *am* American. I've traveled on a U.S. passport all my life. I spent a good portion of every childhood summer in the United States. I lived in the United States from the ages of thirteen to fifteen. I attended university in the United States. I live in the United States now and have for the past twelve years.

The thing is, I don't think of myself as "American." Rather I identify myself as a American-Swiss global nomad with a very European-influenced international background.

Why is this subject so important to me? It has to do with fitting in and belonging, with my intent to be a part of society rather than apart from. It has to do with finding integrity and direction in my experience as a "cultural marginal."

Cultural Marginality

Cultural marginality describes an experience, one typical of global nomads or of others molded by exposure to two or more cultural traditions. Such people do not tend to fit perfrectly into any one of the cultures in which they have lived, but may fit comfortably on the edge, in the margins of each.

Cultural marginality is in and of itself neither bad nor good, although the experience has the potential to be both. It is characterized by the potential for, on the one hand, feeling at home nowhere and, on the other hand, feeling at home everywhere. Whether our cultural marginality hinders or helps us depends on what we do with it. We can allow ourselves to become "encapsulated," trapped by it, or we can learn to use it constructively, as a strategic advantage.

Janet Bennett, co-director of the Intercultural Communications Institute (ICI) and director of the ICI/Antioch master's degree program in intercultural relations, has written a paper titled "Cultural Marginality: Identity Issues in Intercultural Training."[1] In it she discusses two possible responses to marginality: encapsulated and constructive.

Encapsulated Marginality

Those trapped in their marginality tend to be unsure of who they are. As Bennett puts it, they are "buffeted by conflicting cultural loyalties." They surrender their own opinions and concerns to follow somewhat aimlessly the actions of those around them. They may have difficulty making decisions, defining boundaries, identifying personal truths. They often feel alienated, powerless, anxious, angry, and that life is devoid of meaning.

Encapsulated marginals typically experience themselves as isolated: perceiving their circumstances as so unique that they do not, cannot, envision a peer group with whom they can relate. Bennett says, "This captive state can be called 'terminal uniqueness,' for it seems irresolvable to the encapsulated marginal." She adds, "They may report feeling inauthentic all the time, as if any engagement in society is simply role-playing, and there is no way to ever feel 'at home.'" Global nomads may respond by abandoning their international selves in order to try to assimilate into the society in which they find themselves. This process can be exacerbated by others: I remember hearing of one global nomad whose fiancée warned him that he'd have to give up "all that international stuff" if he really wanted to marry her.

Constructive Marginality

Global nomads who are constructive in their marginality also have been buffeted by conflicting cultural loyalties. In struggling to understand themselves, however, they have come to understand their cultural marginality. They have developed a strong sense of who they are. They have a clear commitment to a personal truth and are able, as Bennett says, "to form clear boundaries in the face of multiple cultural perspectives."

Bennett cites a term coined by Muneo Yoshikawa: "dynamic in-betweenness." Dynamic in-betweenness suggests that the constructive marginal is able to move easily and powerfully between different cultural traditions, acting appropriately and feeling at home in each, and in doing so, simultaneously maintaining an integrated, multicultural sense of self. Rather than the "either/or" identity of the encapsulated marginal, constructive marginals experience their movement between cultures as "both/and."

Constructive marginals tend to put their multicultural experiences to good use. Global nomads, for example, come to recognize that the knowledge and skills they have gained through their internationally mobile childhoods can further their personal and professional goals.

Bennett notes that "unlike the encapsulated marginal, the constructive marginal feels authentic and recognizes that one is never not at home in the world." She continued, "This comfort may be partially due to the acknowledgment that one does have a peer group. It is not fellow members of one's [passport] culture, but rather a group of fellow marginals with whom one has more in common than with anyone else." For many global nomads and third culture kids (TCKs), it is when they first discover those terms, first learn about Global Nomads International, that they finally "come home." They can finally name a community to which they fully belong, where they don't need to explain themselves, where their experiences are understood and celebrated.

Nationality and Cultural Marginality

What does all of this have to do with my reaction that spring Sunday in Switzerland when I was introduced as "American?" Such a reaction is certainly not unique to me: many adult global nomads to whom I've posed the question agree that they too have such a reaction when introduced by citizenship.

I think global nomads who don't like to be introduced by citizenship don't like it for two reasons. First, it doesn't adequately describe us. It renders invisible the multiplicity of our experience. It ignores the fact that who we are was shaped through exposure to more than one national culture and by the experience of international mobility.

Second, it renders invisible the work we have done to develop a strong sense of identity as cultural marginals. Many of us first experienced our marginality in a significant way upon reentry to our passport countries. We typically experienced it as something painful and encapsulating. It has taken hard work (even if only that of getting older, and, we hope, wiser) to change our experience of marginality to a constructive one.

A Multicultural Reality

Let me use my own story to illustrate. I was reared to consider myself an American. While my Swiss citizenship always was proudly acknowledged, it was the United States that served as "home base." Summer vacations included short visits to relatives in Switzerland and long visits to relatives in the United States. In Switzerland we went hiking and swimming and did all those things one does on holiday. In the United States we also went to doctors and dentists and did all those things one does at "home" before leaving again for distant lands. When we misbehaved, my siblings and I were reminded that the world's impression of the United States rested upon our actions; we were our country's ambassadors. We went to expatriate-sponsored celebrations of the Fourth of July and to international schools with a heavy American influence. And my parents assumed that my sisters and I would attend university in the United States, as indeed we all eventually did.

Though I was reared to consider myself American, my core identity was formed by peoples and places, sights, sounds, and smells from all over the world. I was born in the United States but left at the age of fourteen months. I lived in ten countries on five continents by age eighteen and moved internationally twelve times by age twenty-two. I attended schools in the French and British systems as well as international schools. We used Urdu, Tamil, Swiss, and Arabic in our family's private language. I celebrated Guy Fawkes Day when we lived in England, received a full series of rabies shots while living in Morocco, and participated in the naming ceremony for my batik teacher's son when we lived in Singapore.

Like me, most global nomads are reared to consider themselves full members of the countries on whose passports they travel. A Nigerian expatriate spouse attending one of my programs a few years ago told me the following story in a voice filled with both frustration and anger. When asked where they were from, each of her children named in turn the country in which he or she was born (Belgium, England, France). Her response, she said, was to say, "No, no, you're Nigerian." Her children, however, had little direct experience of Nigeria—even less than I had had of the United States. Their knowledge of "home" was mediated by their parents, by what news of Nigeria reached the host-country media, and by what they heard host-country nationals and other expatriates say.

Being Nigerian meant little to those young Nigerian global nomads. Indeed, national identity means little to many global nomad children. Some may romanticize their passport country; others may absorb a dislike and mistrust of it. Few really question their identity until they reenter the country they have always considered theirs. I certainly did not question my identity. I was reared to consider myself American, and so I did—until I went "home" to the United States to live.

Reentry and Cultural Marginality

My first reentry took place at the age of thirteen, my next at nineteen. It was a painful experience both times. I learned each time that the Ameircan I was reared to be was not "American" in the way my new peers experienced it. I shared none of the popular knowledge and few of the common experiences. The things I cared about were irrelevant to those around me. I behaved in ways considered "foreign" and spoke with an accent. I felt "terminally unique." We could all have better understood this, I and my American peers, if we didn't all consider me to be "American." I simply didn't fit the U.S. mainstream. I was a cultural marginal. I felt trapped by my difference. In Bennett's term, I was encapsulated by my marginality.

This is a very common description of the global nomad reentry experience. I've worked with several groups of global nomads on issues of reentry. One group was mostly university-age global nomads whose reentry experiences were still very fresh. The other groups consisted of global nomads in their thirties and forties, with some in their fifties and sixties. Without exception, all reported how difficult it had been to be so different. For many, reentry was the first time they realized that they were culturally marginal. It had never been an issue abroad. Once "home," each had to find a precarious balance on the outside edge, on the cultural margin, of the country they had been reared to think of as theirs.

I went abroad twice more, at ages fifteen and twenty-two, each time finding comfort and solace in being someplace where it was obvious to everyone around me that I didn't "belong." I could fit comfortably into the cultural margins because nobody expected me to be in the mainstream. I didn't have to deal with my marginality—it just was.

Developing a Constructive Experience of Marginality

Finally, at age twenty-three, I returned to the United States and was once more confronted with my marginality. I learned over time to fit in by not fitting in. Looking back at university, many of my closest friends were also cultural marginals in their own ways, as are many of my friends now.

I went to graduate school, studied intercultural conflict management, and trained to be a mediator. My studies and subsequent work as a corporate consultant helped me learn to use my marginality constructively, to help me become a part of society rather than apart from it.

I found that my marginality benefited me: It was a professional advantage as well as personally comfortable.

I could move in and out, between and among conflicting parties, building bridges across their differences, but never settling firmly on one side or another, in one place or another. I was introduced in my late twenties to the concept of global nomads by Norma McCaig and David Pollock, and found a community of people with whom I belong. I discovered the field of intercultural communication wherein my international experience and mobile childhood are valued. I function personally and professionally in environments that require me to use my intercultural skills. As I get older I am evolving a personal truth to which I am fully committed, while maintaining my ability to appreciate the truths of others. Moving from encapsulated to constructive marginality was a process, not an event. It was not always comfortable, and it was not conscious at the time. Now I can celebrate my cultural marginality.

What We Can Do

I question whether it is necessary or inevitable that global nomads first experience marginality as encapsulating. As adult global nomads, parents of global nomads, and teachers of global nomads, there are many things we can do together to help internationally mobile children experience their differences as constructive, and avoid or escape from a painful experience with encapsulated marginality.

One of the most important actions we can take is to foster global nomads' multicultural identities. We too often seek to contain our children within a single national identity: French *or* Nigerian, Indonesian *or* American, British *or* Peruvian. Instead, better to acknowledge that nationality is only one part of the international experience. Better to encourage global nomads to develop their identity as global nomads, multicultural people with much to offer a multicultural world. We foster experiences of constructive marginality when we allow people to be all of who they are.

International schools have a role to play here, too: multicultural curriculums; transition programs, programs addressing entry, leave-taking, and reentry; discussion and activity groups addressing global nomad identity issues.

Identifying a peer group can in and of itself be transformative. Introduce global nomads to people with whom they can relate, with whom they can speak about the whole of who they are and feel authentic. Many adult global nomads, talking about how they learned to manage their own reentry experiences, report finding other global nomads (even if they weren't so identified) or joining with foreign students on campus. Indeed the importance of no longer being terminally unique is what leads to membership in organizations such as Global Nomads International and the formation of local global nomad communities around the world.

Bennett argues that the single most important ingredient in building a constructive experience of marginality is developing a sense of one's own truth. Certainly it is valuable to be able to understand different truths as represented in different cultures, to withhold judgment and interpretation. That is part of the global nomad's birthright. At the same time, however, it is important for the adult global nomad to plant his or her feet in personal truth, one not dependent on circumstance.

To be able to say, "This is what I believe, regardless of the cultural context in which I find myself. I may alter my behavior according to changing circumstances, but my truth remains my truth."

As global nomads, we owe it to ourselves and to one another to encourage the experience of constructive rather than encapsulated cultural marginality. There is so much power, so much to celebrate, in the constructive expression of the global nomad experience!

Notes

1. E. Michael Paige, ed., *Education for the Intercultural Experience* (Yarmough, ME: Intercultural Press, 1993).

World Citizens and "Rubber-Band Nationality"
Carolyn D. Smith

CAROLYN DOGGETT SMITH *grew up in a Foreign Service family in the late 1940s and 1950s. She has lived in Italy, Greece, Switzerland, Pakistan, and Vietnam and now works as a freelance editor/writer and book publisher in New York city. She is the author of* The Absentee American: Repatriates' Perspectives on America *and co-editor of* In the Field: Readings on the Field Research Experience.

A FEW YEARS AGO I conducted interviews and distributed questionnaires among a large number of Americans who had spent all or part of their childhood outside the United States. The details of their experiences varied greatly, but the emotional content of their responses was strikingly similar. Almost all expressed an intense feeling of being different from Americans who had not lived overseas during their formative years. Many had made an effort to suppress that feeling and become reintegrated into American society and culture, but many others continued to feel like outsiders—sometimes defiantly so. And almost all the respondents

shared a sense of being something other than, or
more inclusive than, "an American." In this article I explore some of the possible causes and consequences of this expanded sense of national
identity.

> Basically, I consider myself international. I
> feel partial to many cultures and therefore
> am many nationalities in one.

> I feel like a citizen from all over.

> If passports for global citizens or citizens of
> the world were issued, I would probably go
> for one.

The above quotes are typical of the way
Americans who spent some of their childhood
overseas respond to the question "Do you consider yourself an American?" Americans who have
lived overseas in childhood often invent terms for
themselves such as "international Americans,"
"European Americans," or "world citizens," although they will generally agree that they are
"American" in the sense that they are American
citizens. What is the connection between a
multicultural childhood and the feeling that one
is a "world citizen"?

One possible explanation lies in the fact that
Americans growing up overseas often come to see
the United States as another foreign country, one
that they visit from time to time, not their "home."
They enter the United States the way they enter
other countries: as outsiders. They must learn

about American culture in the same way that they must learn about the cultures of the countries in which their parents are stationed. So it should not be surprising that they develop a concept of nationality that lacks clear boundaries.

This is not to say that Americans living overseas cease to think of themselves as Americans. An individual's nationality is learned in early childhood, and it becomes part of the personality. People who become stateless for one reason or another experience a degree of distress that is hard for passport-carrying nationals to imagine; indeed, the passport has been described as a "little identity-book."[1] But for overseas Americans the idea of an "international American" sounds reasonable. You need a passport, of course, but you can expand the sense of nationality to include ties to other countries, particularly those in which you have lived in childhood. In other words, you are an "American" primarily but not exclusively.

Another factor contributing to the sense of being a global citizen is the tendency of young Americans who return for college to become friends with foreign students, feeling more comfortable with others who have, at least to some extent, shared their experience of crossing national and cultural boundaries. Since those students may come from several countries, such friendships provide fertile soil for internationalism. Indeed, repatriates occasionally comment that they could visualize the creation of a world government.

Returnees' sense of having ties to the world as well as to the nation is reflected in the dismay they express at Americans' comparative lack of

interest in world affairs. Journalist Mort Rosenblum, author of *Back Home: A Foreign Correspondent Rediscovers America*, notes that during the
1988 election,

> voters showed interest in the economy, jobs,
> drugs and environment, not 'foreign affairs.'
> No one pointed out that almost everything
> was a foreign affair in today's tiny world.[2]

The reentry experience itself—that is, returning to the United States after a sojourn abroad—
can produce a loosening of the ties of nationality.
This experience is often compared to the reentry of
a spacecraft into the earth's atmosphere. The fact
that reentry often occurs during adolescence is significant, since adolescence is a time when people
are forming their identities. The returnee's "American" identity may receive a rude shock when peers
treat him or her as strange, foreign, or from outer
space. As one returnee puts it,

> Living overseas gave me a feeling of being
> American (obviously) and yet at the same
> time of being out of touch with the USA and
> almost like an outsider who is expected to
> be an insider.

It is interesting to note that Japanese returnees have similar experiences. They are occasionally referred to as "inside-outsiders," meaning a
person who is different and yet must be acknowledged as Japanese. Sometimes they are called
gaijin, "foreigner." And like American returnees

they often find themselves excluded from groups at work and school and learn not to say much about their life overseas. Japanese families seem to share the feeling of U.S. families that spend time overseas—they exist in a kind of limbo, between life overseas and life in Japan.[3]

* * *

I have long been interested in the effects of overseas life on people's concepts of nationality. I am curious about how people feel about their identity as "Americans"—as citizens of the United States and as members of the nation known as America. In exploring this question, it is necessary to distinguish between citizenship and national consciousness. Citizenship is easier to quantify, in that it is represented by a passport. It entails membership in a particular political unit—a nation in this case—and is accompanied by a specific set of rights (civil, political, social) and responsibilities. National consciousness is much broader and hazier, with vast social and psychological ramifications. National consciousness, or the feeling of having a nationality, permeates Americans' relations with people of other nations. It is also a key element of their self-definition, especially when they are living or traveling overseas. In fact, it can become a highly charged emotional issue when an individual faces the risk of losing his or her citizenship (e.g., upon becoming a citizen of another country for purposes of employment there).

The emotional quality of nationality is illustrated by the case of a young American woman who had been a resident of Egypt during much of her childhood. Upon returning to the United States for college, she was required to go through the immigration line at the airport and to take a loyalty oath before she could enter her own country, a procedure that offended her deeply. She refers to herself as a native daughter of the United States despite her family's many years of residence in other countries.

Social-scientific studies of national consciousness define it in various ways, but for our purposes here the description proposed by John Stuart Mill is appropriate. According to Mill, national consciousness is created by

> a community of history and politics and through feelings of pride and shame, joy and grief connected with experiences of the past.[4]

At the same time, however, the members of a nation form

> a community of fate, to a large extent brought together and moulded by historical events and natural factors.

Nor does the individual choose the nation of which he or she is a member—

> Membership in a nation is as a rule not a matter of choice. The great majority of people are born into a nation as into a family.[5]

Our consciousness of our nationality, therefore, is like our consciousness of our sex: Nationality, like sex, is acquired at birth and becomes part of the person's psychological identity. And since national consciousness is shared by all the members of a particular nation, it can be seen as a specific kind of group consciousness, or group solidarity. In fact, some theorists relate national consciousness to gregariousness, as in animals living in herds. That gregariousness consists not only in associating with others but also in excluding outsiders, thereby creating group boundaries and reinforcing group solidarity.[6]

If this is the case, it explains why overseas Americans sometimes experience some conflict related to their sense of nationality. Because they are outside the nation's borders, their ties to the group—that is, to Americans in America—are loosened. The result is a kind of "rubber-band nationality": The overseas American's national consciousness, or sense of self as an American, expands and contracts as he or she moves among different cultural settings. People who feel "European" or "African" while living in foreign countries—and refer to those countries as "home"—can still get tears in their eyes upon seeing the Statue of Liberty or the Golden Gate Bridge.

National consciousness is clearly a psychological quality, but it has a strong cultural underpinning. Sociologist Benedict Anderson explores this cultural dimension in depth in his book *Imagined Communities*. His thesis is that a nation is an imagined community, "imagined" because people feel a sense of kinship with others in the same region who speak the same language and read the same newspapers. It is "an imagined community among a specific assemblage of fellow-readers." Thus for Anderson the nation is essentially a cultural artifact based primarily on shared language.[7] And if that is the case, it is easy to see how exposure to other cultures could result in a loosening of the individual's ties to a single nationality—in effect, the person becomes able to envision being part of several "imagined communities."

"Rubber-band nationality" among those who live overseas for a considerable length of time is promoted by the process of adaptation to foreign cultures. Adaptation—especially through proficiency in the host-country language—brings with it greater acceptance of those cultures. This might begin with cuisine, ways of observing holidays, and other customs (some of which are incorporated into the individual's or family's lifestyle), and eventually extend to more fundamental values. An example of the latter is one respondent's comment that the justice system seems more efficient in Islamic nations, despite the comparative cruelty of some of the punishments. Similar comments are made in relation to punctuality, marital fidelity, and consensus versus majority rule. As anthropologist Dennison Nash points out,

> Progress toward successful adaptation found [the overseas resident] de-emphasizing and even rejecting identifications with Americans and increasingly emulating the hosts.[8]

Those who are most adaptable become cultural chameleons; they have a well-developed capacity for change, suggesting a somewhat weaker attachment to the American identity. Essentially, a new self is formed overseas. Nevertheless, the individual retains many elements of American culture while taking on some of those of the host country. This stretching of cultural values may eventually result in a stretching of the individual's national consciousness.

According to sociologist David Pollock, this global outlook comes at the price of a certain detachment. World citizens are good, objective observers, but they may also be loners because they don't feel that they "belong" anywhere. "I'll never truly be American anymore because of the experiences I've had" is a typical comment.

It is worth noting, also, that nationality makes certain demands on the individual. As one scholar explains,

> A national ideology often leads to a differentiation in the rules of conduct which implies almost two different characters in the same person, a private character in regard to private affairs and a national character in national affairs.[9]

Yet young Americans living overseas are often required to conduct their private activities in such a way as not to reflect adversely on their country—that is, to behave like "little ambassadors." This can engender considerable tension as

the young person is left with no area of life that is
free from scrutiny.

* * *

HOW are people who first live overseas as adults
affected by the experience? An influential study
of overseas Americans described the impact of
overseas life in these words:

> An American working in a foreign country
> must learn to dilute his 'American' outlook,
> not merely in his attitudes and conversa-
> tions, but in his own thinking as well. His
> training should include enough exposure to
> alien ways to ease his culture shock when
> he first goes abroad to live and work, to show
> him in easy stages how relative are the
> American values with which he grew up. For
> in overseas work he will be exposed early
> and often to tests of his cultural empathy.[10]

It is this group that Nash described in his
seminal study *A Community in Limbo*. He referred
to Americans living overseas as "a group of expatriates who were something more than travelers
and something less than immigrants." My interviews indicate that those who go overseas as
adults are less likely to see themselves as "world
citizens" because they are more firmly rooted in
American culture. As Nash noted,

> The psychological kinship with one's fellow
> nationals ... tends to become clearer when

abroad. One ... begins to realize that all of them (including oneself) come out of the same national mold."

Under such conditions American identity becomes an important reference point and furloughs or home leave are eagerly anticipated.

Upon returning home, however, adult returnees note that living overseas has caused them to develop greater religious and racial tolerance, together with reduced tolerance for some aspects of American culture. Looking at the United States from the outside, they are shocked when it doesn't measure up to the ideals of freedom and equality. As one woman who returned from Saudi Arabia explains,

> It was very difficult to accept glaring deficiencies here 'at home.' I could easily overlook inefficiency, obtuseness, irrationality, prejudice in a foreign country because almost everything was different—and it was not what I identified with. But in America, each social problem seemed to be an affront to democracy and my idea of being an American."

In fact, reentry can be much harder for adults because they are aware of the specific ways in which they differ from those around them, rather than having a vague feeling of being from outer space.

* * *

It is important to bear in mind that not all Americans who live overseas in childhood undergo the kind of "nationality stretch" that I have described. Some live overseas early in childhood and return to the States during elementary school; compared to teenagers and college students, they have less difficulty becoming reintegrated into childhood friendship groups and picking up American cultural traits. Others resist exposure to foreign cultures beyond learning a few words of the language and sampling the cuisine. In a sense, they never really leave the United States.

While adults living overseas may develop an elastic concept of nationality, this depends on the adaptability of the individual. Some Americans are more willing than others to incorporate foreign elements into their lifestyle and may eventually come to think of themselves as "international" citizens—without, however, giving up their primary allegiance to the United States. Others are so overwhelmed by culture shock that they back away from the host country and its people and cling to their Americanness all the more.

As international interdependencies increase and more people have the experience of living and working in other countries, the conditions that contribute to "rubber-band nationality" will be encountered by increasing numbers of people—not just Americans but people of all nations that engage in international trade, education, and diplomacy. As more people think of themselves as "world citizens"—that is, as national consciousness becomes more diffuse and less rigid—perhaps we can hope for the spread of a more global world-view, one more attuned to the benefits to be gained from greater international cooperation. Such an outlook could indeed pave the way toward "world government," or at least toward more cooperative endeavors in such areas as environmental protection and space exploration. And it suggests that returnees can make an important contribution to the spirit of tolerance within America's borders.

Notes

1.   Harlan Cleveland, Gerard J. Mangone, and John Clarke Adams, *The Overseas Americans* (New York: McGraw-Hill, 1960), p. 143.

2.   Mort Rosenblum, *Back Home: A Foreign Correspondent Rediscovers America* (New York: William Morrow, 1989), p. 441.

3.   Merry White, *The Japanese Overseas: Can They Go Home Again?* (New York: Free Press, 1988).

4.   Quoted in Frederick Hertz, *Nationality in History and Politics* (New York: New Humanities Press, 1950).

5.   Ibid., pp. 13, 27.

6.   Ibid.

7.   Benedict Anderson, *Imagined Communities: Reflections on the Origin and Spread of Nationalism* (New York: Verso, 1983).

8.   Dennison Nash, *A Community in Limbo: An Anthropological Study of an American Community Abroad* (Bloomington: Indiana University Press, 1970), p. 129.

9.   Hertz, pp. 45-46.

10.   Cleveland, Mangone, and Adams, p. xx.

11.   Nash, p, 34.

Where Will I Build My Nest? The Multicultural Third Culture Kid

David C. Pollock

DAVID POLLOCK became interested in working with transcultural kids and global nomads while a college student in the early 1960s. Initially his work was with missionary kids, but in the mid-1980s he began working with young people in Foreign Service, military, and international business families.

Pollock is executive director of Interaction, Inc., which was cofounded by him in 1968. Interaction is designed to serve as both a catalyst and a resource in working with TCKs and their families. It provides seminars for parents and teachers and consults with organizations on preparing children for overseas experiences. Pollock travels extensively to provide on-site seminars for young people, their parents, and faculty and staff of international schools.

HIS MOTHER WAS CAMBODIAN, his father was Swedish. They communicated with each other in French. He had lived in five Pacific Rim countries but had never visited Cambodia, nor had he ever visited Europe. The majority of his first eighteen years had been spent in Hong Kong, but he had been in a so-called international school in Japan for his final two years of high school. Though never having been in the United States, he felt a sense of identity because of his relationship to North American students. As a high school senior he had been accepted at a U.S. university. The next four years of his life seemed secure until a phone call came from his father. His father's business had collapsed, and his dad had called to tell him that he would be able to finance one year of college and after that the young man would be on his own. With tears he asked me, "Where will I build my nest?"

She teaches in an international school in a country unrelated to any of her roots or history. She was raised in Hawaii by a Chinese mother and a Korean father. Her appearance is very Chinese, her name is Korean, her first language is English, and she speaks enough Cantonese and Korean to understand comments made about her when she is among people who speak those languages. Her citizenship is Korean. "After someone said to me, 'Why don't you go where you belong,'" she said, "I didn't have any idea where that would be."

As an introduction to a day-long seminar for students from five universities, I asked participants to tell us their names, the list of places they had lived in for at least six months, and something unique about themselves. A faculty member from one of the universities, who had come in hope of answering some questions about his own globally nomadic past, responded. His list of habitations sounded like the table of contents of an atlas.

"I'm a freak" was his unique characteristic. My inward response was pain for a person who felt that his multicultural upbringing had made him so disconnected from the rest of the population that he was a freak.

These three people represent a growing subgroup known as third culture kids. The lifestyle of these global nomads usually includes both high mobility and the influences of multiple cultures. Their multicultural experiences have a variety of influences on these growing young people. For some, their bicultural or multicultural parentage adds another level to the challenge of cultural identity.

TCKs' world view is affected early in their development as they become aware of differences in behavior, language, customs, and traditions. They usually are open and accepting of differences and may even be a bit uneasy in settings where everyone looks and acts similarly. These different influences make their mark on behavior patterns such as how and what one may eat, what and how celebrations take place, and how the family functions, including how parents carry out their roles as teachers, disciplinarians, and protectors. Cultural forms such as housing, neighborhoods, class distinction, art, and music may vary significantly from the parents' culture, removing the child from the strict observance of that culture and creating a sense of uncertainty for the parent.

Many TCKs give evidence of their awareness of cultural difference very early in their development. They see the "home" culture as a setting in which "we" do things differently than "they" do in either the passport culture or the host culture. "We" in our family are different from our surrounding communities but similar to other "between" families. The difference may not be seen as being good or bad, but simply as different.

How the individual responds to and develops under these influences depends on several overlapping and interrelated factors. These factors include the host culture or cultures, the home culture or cultures (if parents are from differing cultural backgrounds), the amount of time spent in each of the above, the agency by which the family is sponsored, the school or schools attended by the young person, and the family itself. Perhaps the biggest factor, however, is the unique personality and perceptions of the individual himself or herself. The response to the TCK experience may vary greatly from one child to another even in the same family, creating a sense of isolation for some.

The entire global community is experiencing the impact of high mobility from country to country and from culture to culture. Globally mobile people from cultures having very clear cultural values and behaviors are most aware of that impact. People from carefully defined cultures such as those of Korea, Ghana, or Peru find that third culture kids returning to their home community face a mammoth identity crisis. Speaking both the mother tongue and the other language or languages with an accent sets them apart in every location. In the "home" culture the deficits in language are a basis for judging the individual to be lacking in mental skills. The generation gap between many

TCKs and their parents, who expect that their children will maintain their cultural identity, and the criticisms of monocultural grandparents as well as other relatives and friends, create an even greater gap from the home community.

In search of cultural identity, consciously or unconsciously, TCKs place themselves in a category that enables them to maintain some sense of cultural equilibrium, even if only temporarily. The abundance of variables and influences mentioned above creates shades and mixes of impact, but I have identified four basic categories that represent various combinations of looking and thinking alike

		LOOK	
		+	-
T H I N K	+	Look like Think like MIRROR	Look different Think like ADOPTED
	-	Look like Think differently HIDDEN IMMIGRANT	Look different Think differently FOREIGNER

or differently. Those categories are "the mirror," "the adopted one," "the hidden immigrant," and "the foreigner" (see chart).

The Mirror

THIS response occurs when TCKs look like the majority of the people in the host culture and think like that community. Sometimes a predisposition toward compatibility, born of experience or temperament, opens the way for the TCK to be a reflection of the host culture. Some individuals entering a new culture may feel so in tune with the host community that they wonder why they were not born there. In other cases the TCK was indeed born in the culture or was raised in it from a very early age and has a native commitment to that culture. Yet in other situations the TCK enters the host culture at a later stage of development and is powerfully influenced by that community. Attending national schools is often a major influence in this scenario, since schooling is the means by which one generation communicates its culture to the next.

It is important that parents placing their children in the education system of another culture recognize this powerful influence in the child's life. The parent needs to clearly answer the question, "Is it all right with me for my child to become whatever is characteristic of this host culture, or of the culture that dominates the school?" A more pointed question may be, "Is it all right for my grandchildren to be a part of this culture and live

with my child in this country?" These questions
need to be asked early on. To decide when one's
child is seventeen or eighteen that one does not
approve of the adopted community and culture and
does not want the child to marry into it is not only
unkind but destructive. This is not to say that the
school experience and the possible results are not
all right. It is to say, however, that the parents need
to settle this question in their own minds and stand
behind the decision in support of the child.

The American young person in France, the
Nigerian child in Kenya, the Brazilian student in
Puerto Rico, the Japanese TCK in Korea, or the
Norwegian in an American school in Papua, New
Guinea, may assume an identity that is very dif-
ferent from their country of origin, intensified by
their similar appearance to the majority of people
in the host culture or immediate environment.

The Adopted One

THE six-year-old English boy held his father's
hand as they walked along the street in Taipei toward the Chinese school he attended. As they ap-
proached the corner of the street in view of the
school he freed his hand and, looking up, said,
"I'll go from here alone. I don't want the others to
know my father is not Chinese." Children raised
in a multicultural setting, unless reminded by others or forced through circumstances to recognize
their racial characteristics, do not often think of
physical features as different. Surrounded by others of different appearance from early childhood

makes little difference because their thinking is in tune with that of their companions.

Language, including accent, may be in harmony with that of the surrounding group, and so communication of thought and feeling is facilitated. Thinking like members of the host culture becomes a natural part of the individual's experience. Given the flow of communication, the difference in appearance may mean little. Friends may forget, or at least minimize, the visual difference while responding to similarities in viewpoint, humor, values, and life philosophy.

For many TCKs the "look different, think alike" characteristic may relate not to members of the host culture but to others in the expatriate community, especially those who dominate the so-called international school they attend. The Korean family living in Ecuador with children attending the North American dominated international school may work diligently to maintain their Korean language, but the child is also learning Spanish for local survival and English for academic and social survival. If the majority of life is spent in activities connected with the school, the child will tend to become more American than Ecuadorian. Once again the school plays a key role in the cultural development of the young person.

All too often, however, the young person thinking like but appearing different from members of the community in which he or she is growing up is suddenly faced with the reality that the physical difference creates separations in the adult community. What was overlooked as children becomes a point of division as adults. Passports also play a role in forcing adult TCKs to live in places where they look like the majority but do not think like them. This setting produces what we have come to call the "hidden immigrant."

The Hidden Immigrant

THIS is a person who looks like the majority but thinks differently than others in that community. This may occur in two ways. First, one may live in a host culture in which race and ethnicity are similar to one's own. If the individual does not speak, he or she may be considered part of the local community. Opening one's mouth, however, may reveal not only limitations in language skills or a telltale accent, but thoughts and values that are incompatible with those of the host culture. The TCK in such a situation may live with a sense of alienation or isolation even when people of the host culture attempt to reach out in acceptance.

The second way the sense of being a hidden immigrant is experienced is when one enters one's own culture having developed as a TCK with a variety of viewpoints, values, and philosophies that differ from those of the majority in one's home culture. Not only may the TCK be greeted with a less than receptive attitude by citizens of the country of origin, but he or she may be less than positive toward the positions and performances of people in that country. One Asian TCK expressed her response to this experience when she said, "I think I am more comfortable being a foreigner in a foreign country than being a coated stranger in my own country."

The Foreigner

THE TCK who looks different from and continues to think differently than those in the dominant culture is a perpetual foreigner. The layers of influence mentioned earlier (parents, agency, schools, expatriate community, personality, and experience of the individual, etc.) serve as particular controls in keeping the TCK from becoming thoroughly influenced by and molded to the dominant culture of his or her environment.

Though many TCKs have a sense of being at home everywhere and nowhere, some find that they are not at home in the host culture. Though this may be uncomfortable for some, it may make the anticipation of returning to a "home" culture somewhat less stressful. However, two things need to be kept in mind for such individuals. First of all, persons living as foreigners in the host culture may have an unrealistic sense of their ability to fit easily into their home culture or a culture they believe fits them. Actually moving to the place where they anticipate being at home may result in the painful experience of either not being accepted by those in that community or being shocked to discover that they do not fit or even want to fit. Both experiences may occur.

Greta grew up in Indonesia and attended an American-operated international school.

Though the population was multicultural, the faculty and dominant influence were definitely American. In her first year as a university student in North America she wrote:

> I think the Netherlands has a greater place in my heart than I like to admit. It used to be my home for the first five years of my life. It was my own country, my language, my heritage. During our first term in Indonesia I idealized Holland. I didn't like Indonesia and I didn't like the America all my friends talked so fondly about. Dutch was my mother tongue and my English was shaky. I looked at pictures, read letters from my grandparents, remembered the good times at home, and looked forward to returning. The Netherlands seemed perfect.

Upon returning to Europe, Greta discovered that she had changed greatly in that three-year period. The beautiful memories could not be reconstructed: The people weren't as delightful as she had pictured them, and she was accused of speaking with an American accent and of being more American than Dutch. In an attempt to belong somewhere she concluded that she was more American than anything else and entered an American university. In a very short time she wrote, "The honeymoon is over and I realize I am not American either." Like the young man in Japan, her question is, "Where will I build my nest?"

The second issue to be kept in mind for those who fit the "foreigner" description is that being different may become an important aspect of personal identity. The high visibility of looking different from the majority in the host culture may carry with it recognition and in some situations the possibility of special consideration or privilege. To be like everyone else may be a source of disappointment and frustration. Returning to your passport country may result in your being a "coated stranger" or hidden immigrant even if you were a "foreigner" in that last place of residence.

The TCK of multicultural parentage often faces these issues with the extra twist of returning to a passport country that is labeled by at least one of the parents as "home," yet by appearance they will not be readily admitted to that country. The legal right to be in that country in no way guarantees acceptance by others, and the barrier of difference in physical characteristics may be a high one. In such situations individuals need extra understanding, support, and closeness from the nuclear family. Parents must assume responsibility beyond that of others with a simpler profile. Being available to bring comfort may be far more important than giving the good advice to "get out there and prove yourself and all will be well." Obviously encouragement is important, but without empathy and comfort the aloneness and despair of the young person is intensified. Helping a young person to be tough in a tough world does not preclude the need and importance of protection and warmth from the parents. Since the parents' decision has led to the tension, both mother and father need to contribute to the easing of that pressure. Family should be safe and comforting.

Supporting the Multicultural TCK

THERE are several things parents can do to support their multicultural TCKs in both their adjustment and their development. Recognizing differences in situations and personalities, the "how" of accomplishing this will vary from family to family and even from person to person. The individual will ultimately determine his or her own identity, but parents can contribute to the process.

AFFIRM CULTURAL IDENTITY

It is critical to maintain contact with one's own culture through teaching children about that culture using both formal means, including school, and informal means. Geography, history, literature, and music should be part of this teaching from very early ages. The respect for and enjoyment of one's cultural heritage is caught from example rather than taught. This is not to imply exclusivity but rather the healthy mix of one's own cultural heritage with that of the host or dominant culture. Parents need to be warned that insistence on exclusivity usually has the opposite effect.

   Appropriate respect for one's culture and country involves acknowledgment of the positive character and contributions made by that culture. Patriotism is not the same as nationalism. Patriotism allows for the approval of the positive factors as well as criticism of the negative ones. Real patriotism involves the desire and attempt to see positive change in one's own country for its good. TCKs may see their home culture through the eyes of the host culture, the international culture, or simply from the vantage point of being outside looking in. To be able to express opinions about the undesirable aspects as well as the good allows the person to come to a healthy, balanced view of one's roots rather than being the constant critic or the perpetual defender.

The multicultural TCK should be encouraged to know, respect, and delight in all of the parts of his or her heritage. Traditions of both parents, including holidays, should be observed, even if in limited ways, both for the information gained about the culture and for the celebration of the culture. Appropriate pride in one's culture, not arrogance, should be encouraged. Inviting others to celebrate special occasions, experience food and art, and learn about one's origins permits a family to be inclusive while affirming their heritage.

It is critical that contact with families in the "home" country be nurtured. This nurturing begins before leaving the home culture by building those relationships. Before departure parents and children should endeavor to resolve any conflicts with those being left, reaffirm their love and commitment to them, and say farewell in appropriate ways. Regular contact with family and friends in the home culture is imperative. Ease in reconnecting with one's family, community, and culture is enhanced when people from home are able to visit the globally nomadic family in their foreign habitat. Understanding is usually improved when someone from home serves as a bridge because they have shared the cross-cultural experience.

At the heart of the affirmation of one's cultural identity is the development and mastery of language. Where there are two "mother tongues" in bicultural families, both should be learned and honored. I have observed bilingual families in which the father-child communication was in one language and the mother-child conversation was in another. This consistency prevented confusion and produced a multilingual family able to communicate to a large extent with relatives in both cultures as well as with each other.

One bilingual family resolved the issue of when to speak which language by declaring that the mother tongue would be spoken as soon as anyone entered the family home. As soon as the family members crossed the threshold on their way into the community they switched to the language of the culture in which they lived, worked, and were being educated. When they stepped into the house, the home language was used except when guests were present.

Every child deserves to have a mother tongue in which the most important thoughts and deepest concerns can be expressed. For some families in some settings this is easier than for others, but it is a goal that is important to one's cultural identity as well as to one's future adjustment in culture, community, and career.

AFFIRM THE TCK IDENTITY

All too often parents are not fully aware that the decision they have made to move and/or marry cross-culturally will produce children whose development will be very different from their own. In these situations the statement "when I was your age" is irrelevant apart from its historical significance. When the parent from a monocultural background was growing up, the issues of identity were very different. Often the starting point for affirming the TCK identity is the revelation to the parents that implicit in their decisions about marriage, children, career, and where to live was the decision to produce a TCK who would be deeply influenced by the culture(s) in which they have lived. The second step is the recognition that being a TCK is not a disease, does not necessitate therapy, and is not something that one can or should "get over." The TCK is not a cultural ugly duckling. He or she is the product of a multicultural experience that can broaden one's life and produce a variety of desirable abilities.

Parents need to realize, however, that the many benefits of the transcultural upbringing as seen from their adult perspective may not be regarded as enthusiastically by every child. As one adult TCK, an experienced mental health professional, said to me, "The child has no choice in the matter of being uprooted, sees nothing to be gained by it and everything to lose." The impact of mobility on many TCKs may overshadow what one might like to celebrate. The grief and insecurity produced by the loss of that which brings a sense of belonging, delight, and well-being must be addressed in order to open the way to develop and release the potential of the TCK experience. While affirming the value of the transcultural upbringing, parents must be prepared to address the issues of grief from the many losses resulting from mobility.

The high mobility and multicultural exposure and development of the TCK results in a sense of marginality in any and all settings. Belonging nowhere and everywhere is a normal, predictable result. The TCK may be victimized by that marginality as he or she struggles with alienation, powerlessness, and confusion. However, with support and help the TCK may use the richness of his or her life experience to become a cultural guide for others, bringing understanding and harmony in intercultural relations because of knowledge, understanding, and skills constructed on the third culture foundation. Parents, sponsoring agencies, and educational institutions do well to develop supporting communities with services to assist in adjustment, decision-making, and career development as well as support through the more difficult periods in a TCK's life. In a multicultural world, the TCK of any age may play an important role that no thinking community can ignore.

For many people the question "Where are you from?" has many reasonable answers. "Where do you belong?" may be more difficult to answer. "Where will I build my nest?" may still haunt some adult TCKs, but they should find in the international community understanding, support, and assistance in using their TCK experience for their satisfaction and for the good of everyone around them. Understanding and specific action to affirm both the culture or cultures of origin and the "third culture" identity are critical to the adjustment of those who wrestle with these questions.

At the end of the day-long seminar for university students, the professor said, "I have one more comment. Do you remember that I said my uniqueness was that I am a freak? Because of what I have learned today and because of being with all of you I know I am not a freak." Finding an identity and a place to belong should be the experience of every TCK.

SELECTED BIBLIOGRAPHY

Austin, Clyde N. *Cross-Cultural Reentry: An Annotated Bibliography.* Abilene, TX: Abilene Christian University Press, 1983.

Austin, Clyde N. *Cross-Cultural Reentry: A Book of Readings.* Abilene, TX: Abilene Christian University Press, 1986.

Bell, Linda. *Hidden Immigrants: Legacies of Growing Up Abroad.* Notre Dame, IN: Cross Cultural Publications, 1996.

Bloomfield, Katherine M. *The Impact of Overseas Living on Adolescent Identity Formation.* Northampton, MA: Smith College School for Social Work, 1983.

Eakin, Kay Branaman. *The Foreign Service Teenager—At Home in the U.S.: A Few Thoughts for Parents Returning with Teenagers.* Washington, DC: Overseas Briefing Center, Foreign Service Institute, U.S. Department of State, May 1988.

Lewis, Tom J., and Robert E. Jungman, eds. *On Being Foreign: Culture Shock in Short Fiction.* Yarmouth, ME: Intercultural Press, 1986.

McCluskey, Karen, ed. *Notes from a Traveling Childhood: Readings for Internationally Mobile Parents and Children.* Washington, DC: Foreign Service Youth Foundation, 1994.

Pollock, David, and Ruth E. Van Reken. *Growing Up Among Worlds.* Yarmouth, ME: Intercultural Press, forthcoming.

Seaman, Paul. *Paper Airplanes in the Himalayas: Reconstructing a Missionary Childhood.* Unpublished manuscript.

Smith, Carolyn D. *The Absentee American: Repatriates' Perspectives on America.* Bayside, NY: Aletheia Publications, 1994.

Stonequist, Everett V. *The Marginal Man: A Study in Personality and Culture Conflict.* New York: Russell and Russell, 1937.

Storti, Craig. *The Art of Crossing Cultures.* Yarmouth, ME: Intercultural Press, 1992.

Van Reken, Ruth E. *Letters Never Sent.* Indianapolis, IN: "Letters," 1988.

Wertsch, Mary Edwards. *Military Brats: Legacies of Childhood in the Fortress.* Bayside, NY: Aletheia Publications, 1996.

White, Merry. *The Japanese Overseas: Can They Go Home Again?* New York: Plenum Press, 1988.

See also the works cited in the Notes at the ends of selections.

ORGANIZATIONS OF
INTEREST TO RETURNEES

Around the World in a Lifetime (AWAL)
c/o FSYF
P.O. Box 39185
Washington, DC 20016

A social organization for Foreign Service teens. Teens overseas learn about life in the United States through a monthly newsletter; teens in the United States attend monthly meetings.

Global Nomads International
2001 O St., N.W.
Washington, DC 20036

A volunteer organization that promotes the welfare of current and former internationally mobile families and individuals through literature, conferences, and education.

Mu Kappa International
P.O. Box 1388
De Soto, TX 75115

A fraternal association whose purpose is to help missionary kids in their cultural transitions and to promote growth, unity, and Christian fellowship among chapter members.

Overseas Brats
P.O. Box 29805
San Antonio, TX 78229

A nonprofit organization of overseas alumni comprising former dependents of U.S. military, government, and civilian personnel; assists in referring overseas alumni to their respective reunion committees or organizations.

INDEX